Would you like to learn to be a better baker?

We know that so many people watch *The Great British Bake Off* for the tips and techniques you pick up – not only from the judges, but from watching the bakers too. We wanted to distil that knowledge into a library of cookbooks that are specifically designed to take you from novice to expert baker. Individually, each book covers the skills you will want to perfect so that you can master a particular area of baking – everything from cakes to bread, sweet pastries to pies.

We have chosen recipes that are classics of each type, and grouped them together so that they take you on a progression from 'Easy does it' through 'Needs a little skill' to 'Up for a challenge'. Put together, the full series of books will give you a comprehensive collection of the best recipes, along with all the advice you need to become a better baker.

The triumphs and lessons of the bakers in the tent show us that not everything works every time. But I hope that with these books as your guide, we have given you a head start towards baking it better every time!

Linda Collister
Series Editor

THE GREAT BRITISH
BAKE OFF®
— BAKE IT BETTER —

PUDDINGS
& DESSERTS

Jayne Cross

HODDER &
STOUGHTON

Contents

BAKE IT BETTER
Baker's Guide

BAKE IT BETTER
Recipes

Easy does it   42

Welcome bakers!

What better way to end a meal than with a home-made pudding or dessert? Well, here are 40 delicious recipes to get you baking.

As well as being great bakes, the recipes have been carefully chosen to teach you all the key techniques, such as rubbing in, creaming, whisking and folding that will not only help you to make better puddings and desserts but will improve all of your baking.

Start with the 'Easy does it' section to master the basics with recipes like Spiced Plum Crumble and Pear and Chocolate Upside-down Cake. As your confidence grows, move on to those recipes that 'Need a little skill' – Pineapple Tarte Tatin, Profiteroles with Salted Caramel and Chocolate Sauce or Brandy Snaps with Oranges in Caramel. The more you bake the sooner you'll be 'Up for a challenge', whisking both sponge and meringue for a Baked Alaska and testing your puff pastry skills with Millefeuilles.

The colour strip on the right-hand side of the page tells you at a glance the level of difficulty of the recipe (from one spoon for easy to three spoons for a challenge), and gives you a helpful checklist of the skills and special equipment you will use.

Before you begin, take a look at the Baker's Guide at the beginning of the book. This will introduce you to the most important ingredients, tell you what equipment you need to get started (just a bowl, a spoon and a baking dish will do in some cases) and explain some of the terms and techniques in more detail.

Puddings can be a simple affair to round off a midweek family meal, or a stunning dinner-party dessert to impress your friends. It's amazing what you can bake when you set your mind, bowl and spoon to it – so let's get baking.

HOW TO USE THIS BOOK

SECTION 1: BAKER'S GUIDE
Read this section before you start baking.

The Baker's Guide contains key information on ingredients (pages 10–15), equipment (pages 16–21) and skills (pages 22–37) relevant to the recipes in the book.

Refer to the Baker's Guide when you're baking if you want a refresher on a particular skill. In the recipes, the first mention of each skill is highlighted in bold.

SECTION 2: RECIPES
Colour strips on the right-hand side and 1, 2 or 3 spoons show the level of difficulty of the recipe. Within the colour strips you'll find helpful information to help you decide what to bake: Hands-on time; Baking time; Makes/serves; Special equipment and the key skill used.

Refer back to the Baker's Guide when a skill is highlighted in bold in the recipe if you need a reminder.

Try Something Different options are given where the recipe lends itself to experimenting with other ingredients or decorations.

BAKE IT BETTER

Baker's Guide

Ingredients

There is a huge variety of puddings and desserts that you can make, whether cake-based puddings, filled pastry tarts, or fruit or chocolate desserts. However, there are some key ingredients that you will use again and again. Knowing a bit about these ingredients before you start will help you to understand how they work and so avoid problems and become a better baker. This list will help you through the process of buying, storing and using the main ingredients that feature in the recipes in this book.

BUTTER

All the recipes in this book use **unsalted butter**. It is the butter of choice for most bakers as it has a mild and delicate flavour and gives you the option to add salt or not to suit your tastes. Unsalted butter usually contains less whey than **salted butter** and so gives a more even colour to your bake. You can substitute salted butter for unsalted if that is all you have to hand, just remember not to add any additional salt if the recipe calls for it.

Each recipe specifies the temperature that the butter needs to be at. For example, for a **creamed sponge** or **pâte sucrée** the butter needs to be soft and so should be at room temperature so that it can be smoothly incorporated into the sugar. If you need to **rub in** the butter, for example when you are making a crumble topping or shortcrust pastry, the butter needs to be chilled and diced to rub in effectively.

Butter should be kept well wrapped in the fridge and away from foods with strong flavours as it can absorb those flavours, which will affect the taste of your bakes. It can also be frozen for up to a month; defrost it in the fridge before using.

CHOCOLATE

Where possible, use the best chocolate that you can find as it will have a big impact on the flavour and finish of your puddings. One of the most important things to look for in the ingredients list on a bar of chocolate is the percentage. This refers to cocoa solids and can be anything up to 100 per cent. The rest should be made up from only sugar, milk powder (for milk chocolate) and sometimes a binding agent. Good-quality chocolate is widely available in supermarkets and you can also buy ready-chipped chocolate from specialist online suppliers. Chocolate should be stored well wrapped in a cool, dark cupboard and away from any strong-flavoured foods. Keep an eye on the best-before date. You should always chop chocolate into pieces before melting to help it to melt evenly and prevent it from scorching.

Dark chocolate is the most widely used chocolate in baking, and those that contain around 70 per cent of cocoa solids give the best flavour. Those with a lower cocoa content can be too sweet, and those that are higher than 75 per cent are generally too bitter for most recipes.

Milk chocolate has a milder and sweeter taste than dark, but again you should use one that has as high a cocoa content as possible (30 per cent and above is good). This not only has a better flavour but will also set slightly firmer.

White chocolate doesn't contain any cocoa solids, just cocoa butter, and so it is that content that you need to look out for. Again, buy the best quality that you can as a lot of the cheaper ones contain no cocoa butter at all and are far too sweet. Ideally, something with 30 per cent or higher cocoa butter is best, but bear in mind that as white chocolate has a higher fat content than both dark and milk chocolate, it will set slightly less firmly.

COCOA POWDER
A dark, unsweetened powder made from pure cocoa that has had nearly all of the cocoa butter removed. It has a bitter and strong flavour that adds a great chocolate taste to your baking and is particularly useful where you want the flavour of chocolate without the added moisture of melted chocolate, for example when making chocolate pastry. Don't ever use drinking chocolate in place of cocoa as that has had dried milk and sugar added to it and so will greatly affect the taste and performance of your bake.

CREAM
Always use the type of cream specified in the recipe as each one has a different fat content and so this can affect the end result.

Single cream has at least 18 per cent butterfat and is good for pouring, but it is not suitable for whipping.

Double cream has at least 48 per cent butterfat content and whips well when chilled, making it ideal for recipes such as the Cherry and Chocolate Knickerbocker Glory and Raspberry Trifle (see pages 92 and 108). In its unwhipped state it is also used to make ice cream, cheesecakes and panna cotta. Don't use the extra-thick double cream as a substitute as this has been heat-treated and so won't whip; nor is it suitable for making ganache. It's only really

to be used for spooning from the pot rather than in baking.

Whipping cream has at least 35 per cent butterfat and is ideal for, yes you guessed it, whipping. As with double cream this whips best when chilled.

Buttermilk is traditionally the by-product of butter-making, but it is now made by adding a bacterial culture to skimmed milk and so is sold as 'cultured buttermilk'. It has a slightly sour and acidic taste and is used to make scones (see Rhubarb Cobbler, page 54), as well as to add lightness and flavour to cakes.

Soured cream is made by adding a culture to single cream and so has the same 18 per cent fat content, but with a distinct sour tang. It is widely used in both chilled and baked cheesecakes (see Key Lime Cheesecake and Baked Vanilla Cheesecake, pages 60 and 100).

Crème fraîche is the French version of soured cream but is a lot thicker, and has a milder and richer flavour. It makes a great accompaniment to puddings in place of regular cream.

EGGS
All the recipes in this book use medium-sized eggs (about 62–65g each). The size of egg you use in baking is important as it works in ratio with all of your other ingredients, meaning that if you use a larger or smaller egg it could well affect the end result. You may find you need more or less liquid to bind your ingredients, your bake may need a shorter or longer time in the oven, or it may not rise properly.

Store eggs in the fridge, pointed-side down as this helps the white cover the yolk and so stops it from drying out. Keep them in the box you bought them in as this helps keep out flavours from other foods in the fridge and store them in the cooler main body of the fridge, not the door. Spare egg whites will keep for 3–4 days in the fridge, in a sealed container, or for up to a month in the freezer. Label them with the date and quantity, and always defrost thoroughly before using. Don't freeze egg yolks.

Eggs should be at room temperature when used in baking as they give a greater volume when beaten and so you should take them out of the fridge for 30–60 minutes before using. If you forget, you can warm them in a bowl of lukewarm water for about 10 minutes.

EXTRACTS AND FLAVOURINGS

Try to avoid the synthetic flavourings that are usually cheaper as they can add a 'fake' taste to your bake.

Vanilla extract is widely available and as its name implies is extracted from vanilla pods, whereas vanilla flavouring or essence is chemically produced. The flavour of extract is much stronger than essence and so although more expensive you only need a small amount. Whole **vanilla pods** are used to infuse cream, custard and ice cream, and if split and the seeds removed, add a lovely fleck of vanilla as well as flavour. **Vanilla bean paste** is made from the seeds of vanilla pods and gives a more concentrated flavour than vanilla extract.

Ground spices should be stored in a cool, dark place in screw-top jars to ensure they keep their colour and flavour. Try to use

them within a few months of opening while they are still fresh.

Stem ginger in syrup is a great addition to your store cupboard. It keeps well and you can use both the balls of ginger diced into small pieces or the syrup from the jar to add a ginger kick (see Apple and Stem Ginger Lattice Tart and Steamed Stem Ginger Puddings with Custard, pages 86 and 90).

FLOUR

Only use fresh flour as old flour can really affect the flavour and performance of your bake. Store opened bags in storage jars, plastic food boxes or bags to stop the flour from getting damp, and don't add new flour to old in your jars. Aim to use it within a month of opening or by its best-before date.

Wheat flours are the most frequently used in baking. **Plain flour** is the one most commonly used in pastries and biscuits. **Self-raising flour** is made by adding baking powder to plain flour and is usually used in the creamed method of cake-making to give the rise to the cakes. You can make your own self-raising flour by adding 4 teaspoons baking powder to 225g plain flour. **Strong white bread flour** is used in puff pastry as it contains more gluten and so the dough has more elasticity, which gives a better flakiness to the pastry. **Cornflour** is an ideal flour to use as a thickening agent as it blends to a smooth cream with liquid and so is used when making sauces such as custard and crème pâtissière.

Gluten-free flours are now much more readily available and are usually made from a combination of rice, potato, tapioca, maize, chickpea, broad bean, white sorghum or buckwheat flours. Their taste, texture and performance can vary from brand to brand so it's worth trying a few out to see which works best for you. Some include xantham gum (which comes in powdered form) and this improves the texture of both cakes and pastry. So check that the flour you are using has it; if not, add 1 teaspoon xantham gum to 150g flour. Also check that your baking powder is gluten free.

GELATINE

Gelatine is made from animal collagen and is available in leaf and powdered form. The recipes in this book use leaves, as they tend to result in a clearer, firmer-set jelly. Both the powder and leaves are dissolved in water before combining with the rest of your mixture. The leaves are soaked first to soften them, then the water squeezed out. Vegetarian alternatives are now readily available, such as **agar-agar**, which is a seaweed extract. Most alternatives can be used interchangeably with gelatine, but check the instructions on the packet for specific advice. For example, agar-agar needs to be boiled until it fully dissolves.

GROUND ALMONDS

Ground blanched almonds are great for adding flavour and texture to pie fillings or pastry. They can go off quite quickly as they are very oily and so they should be stored in a cool, dark place in an airtight container; label the container so that you use them before the best-before date.

ICING SUGAR is a fine, white powdered sugar that dissolves readily and so is ideal for whisking into cream for cake fillings and for making buttercream. It's also used in sweet pastries such as **rich shortcrust pastry** and

pâte sucrée to keep the texture of the dough nice and smooth. Sift it well to remove any lumps before using.

MARGARINES AND SPREADS

These are made from vegetable oils, with added salt and flavourings. Some are made specifically for baking but are not used for the recipes in this book. Where butter is specified it is best not to substitute with margarine or a spread as the flavour will differ, as will the water content, so they are unlikely to result in a successful bake.

POLENTA

Polenta is a golden yellow Italian cornmeal made from ground dried maize and is therefore gluten free. It can be finely or coarsely ground but the most widely available polenta is quick-cook polenta, which is used in the Orange and Polenta Cake with Cranberry Sauce (see page 66). Its slightly grainy texture enhances the texture of the cake as well as adding a lovely colour.

RAISING AGENTS

Some bakes need the addition of a chemical raising agent to help them to rise: the two most common are bicarbonate of soda and cream of tartar. Baking powder is a mixture of both, and if you want you can make your own by mixing 1 teaspoon of bicarbonate of soda with 2 teaspoons of cream of tartar.

Raising agents work by reacting with the moisture in the cake. When heated, they release small bubbles of carbon dioxide and so lighten the texture of the cake. They can be used in flourless cakes to help them rise. Gluten-free baking powder is widely available and so is ideal for such recipes.

SUGAR

There are many types of sugar available and it is important to always use the sugar specified in the recipe as they all behave differently. All sugars should be stored in airtight bags or jars to stop them drying out.

Caster sugar has a fine texture and is the one best used for most cakes and pastries as the grains break down well when beaten with butter or eggs and will also provide a nice smooth pastry. It is also essential for making meringues; its fine texture dissolves easily into the egg whites as you whisk and so produces a smooth and glossy meringue. **Golden caster sugar** is unrefined and so is not as fine but has a richer flavour and slightly deeper colour. **Granulated sugar** has bigger grains and so is best used for dissolving in jams or liquids rather than creaming into mixtures; it can leave a speckled finish on top of your bake.

Brown and muscovado sugars are available in both light and dark and they add a warm colour and toffee or butterscotch flavour when added to bakes or sauces (see Sticky Toffee Pudding, page 68). They can form lumps in storage so sift or press them out before use.

SYRUPS

As with sugar and flour, it's important to use the correct syrup as they can have very different flavours. **Golden syrup** is a pale golden syrup made from sugar cane; it is sweeter than sugar and adds a moist, dense texture to cakes and tarts when used (see Individual Treacle Tarts, page 58). It is sticky and therefore quite tricky to measure out, so use a metal spoon and warm it up first in a mug of hot water so the syrup will slide from the spoon, or sit the whole tin in some just-boiled water. **Maple syrup** is made by boiling down the sap of maple trees to produce a concentrated syrup that is runnier than golden syrup, darker in colour and has a deep, rich flavour.

Equipment

The great thing about baking is that you don't need a whole heap of expensive equipment to get started; most things you will probably already have in your kitchen. Many of the recipes can be made with just a bowl, a wooden spoon and a whisk, but as you progress through the book you will find that there are certain pieces you will need to make your baking more enjoyable and successful. Do check each recipe before you start, so that you know what you need to complete it.

BAKING BEANS

Ceramic baking beans are used for making tarts such as the Fig and Frangipane Tart on page 80, where you blind bake the pastry case before filling to keep the pastry base flat and the sides in place (and to avoid the dreaded soggy bottom). You can always use dried rice or beans instead, but ceramic beans are heavier, hold their heat better and so are a worthwhile investment.

BAKING DISHES

Ovenproof baking dishes, used for many hot puddings and desserts such as crumbles, cobblers and rice pudding, can be made of ceramic or glass and they are generally measured in centimetres or a liquid capacity. If you are unsure of the size of your dish, fill the dish with water and then pour that water into a measuring jug to see how much it holds. As with cake and flan tins it is important to use the correct size of baking dish as the recipe and baking times are based on that size.

BAKING PAPER AND LINERS

Non-stick liners are essential to stop cakes, biscuits and meringues from sticking to tins and trays. A roll of **non-stick baking paper** is the most useful as it can be cut to fit tins and trays of all shapes and sizes. **Silicone baking mats** can be expensive and are not as readily available, but can be re-used, so if looked after properly will last a long time. **Ready-made cake tin liners and discs** for lining the bases of tins will save you a lot of time and effort if you do a lot of baking, and are available from most supermarkets. **Greaseproof paper** is best kept for wrapping cooked bakes as it is water resistant, but its waxy coating doesn't stand up well to heating.

BAKING SHEETS AND TRAYS

A **baking sheet** is flat with just one raised edge, whereas a **baking tray** has raised edges on all sides. Choose sturdy ones that won't buckle when in the oven, as that will ensure your tarts and bakes stay flat and so cook evenly.

Baking sheets are great for cooking tarts on as it is easier to slide them off a flat edge than a raised one. The same goes for thin biscuits such as tuiles and brandy snaps where you need to be able to slide a palette knife under them easily. It is good to have two or three baking sheets so that you can cook whole batches at once.

BAKING TINS

It is important to use the size of tin that is specified in the recipe as the quantities and baking times have been based on that tin size. Ideally, you want to buy solid, heavy-duty tins as they will last longer and give a better, more consistent bake to your cakes. Heavy-duty metal cake tins are the most reliable and durable, but you can also get non-stick metal, heavy aluminium, ceramic and silicone cake tins.

Sandwich tins are the ones most used in cake-making and a pair of round, straight-sided tins, 20cm across and sides 4–5cm high, are the most useful.

Deep round/square cake tins are good for larger, deeper cakes, such as the Orange Polenta Cake (page 66) and are available with either fixed or loose bases. Loose-bottomed tins are the best to get as it is easier to turn the cake out if you can push the base up first.

Springclip tins have a spring release on the side so they are really useful when making cheesecakes or cakes that are more fragile as the sides can be removed easily without fear of damaging the cake. They come in many sizes, but 20cm and 22–23cm are the most frequently used.

Swiss roll tins these are shallow rectangular tins about 2cm high and are usually 20 x 30cm. They are most often used for whisked sponges that are then rolled, such as for the Raspberry Trifle (page 108).

Flan/tart tins are ideal for cooking tarts. A sturdy metal one with a loose bottom is ideal, as it will cook the pastry evenly and will be easier to take your tart out once it's cooked. They come in all shapes and sizes with the most commonly used being 20cm and 23cm diameter. **Tartlet tins** are smaller versions of tart tins and again should be loose-bottomed.

Tarte Tatin tins are specially designed for the job, with a thick base that can withstand cooking on the hob, and sloping sides and a non-stick surface that make it easier for turning the tarte out when it is cooked.

BOWLS

A nest of small, medium and large bowls is useful and easy to store. **Heatproof glass** bowls are the most versatile when it comes to melting chocolate or making custards, as they can be put over pans of simmering water to heat the contents gently – they can also go in the microwave. **Ceramic** bowls are good but can break quite easily and are usually heavier. **Stainless steel** bowls are unbreakable but no good for the microwave. **Plastic** bowls are generally cheaper and some come with rubber bases which means they won't slip as you mix or whisk. They can go in the microwave but some of the thinner cheaper ones might get scratched and damaged by the blades on a hand-held mixer. **Anodised aluminium** bowls are very durable and will last a lifetime but are no good in the microwave.

COOLING RACKS

Wire cooling racks allow the air to circulate around your bakes as they cool, preventing them from going soggy or soft. Large rectangular cooling racks are best as they allow you to cool a batch of biscuits or two cakes at one time. You can use the wire grill pan rack as a stand-in, but the finer wires on a cooling rack work better and are less likely to make indents on your cakes or biscuits.

FOOD-PROCESSOR

A food-processor is not an essential piece of equipment but can prove to be a very useful one. It makes light work of chopping and blending, particularly when blitzing something like hardened caramel. It can also give better results when using the rubbing in method to make pastry, as warm hands are not involved.

KNIVES

A **medium-sized sharp knife,** around 20cm long, will cover you for most purposes, and if you choose a heavy, good-quality blade it should last longer. Hold a knife in your hand before you buy it to check that you like the feel of the handle and that it balances well. A **knife sharpener** is vital to keep your knife sharp and at its best. A **small serrated knife** is useful for peeling and cutting fruit and trimming pastry from the edges of pie dishes. **Palette knives** are good for spreading icings as well as sliding biscuits from baking sheets and removing cakes and tarts from cake tin bases.

Knives are made from different materials. The main ones to consider are stainless steel, which is cheaper but needs to be sharpened regularly; carbon steel, which is more expensive, harder and easier to keep sharp; and ceramic, which is the hardest of all, much lighter and doesn't need sharpening but can chip easily.

LARGE METAL SPOON

A large metal spoon with a long handle is very useful for folding in (page 32) and also for transferring cake mixtures into tins, and cream and meringue into piping bags.

MEASURING JUG

Choose a jug that is heat resistant and microwave safe with clear metric and imperial measures, starting from 50ml if you can find one, otherwise 100ml and going up to 1 or 2 litres. A small jug that has measures from 5ml (1 teaspoon) up to 60ml (4 tablespoons) is also very useful.

MEASURING SPOONS

Everyday teaspoons and tablespoons vary in size enormously and so should not be used for baking. A set of measuring spoons, ideally ranging from ⅛ teaspoon to 1½ tablespoons, is essential to ensure you add the exact amount, especially with raising agents, spices and liquids. Try to find a set with narrow ends that will fit into small spice jars and bottles. All spoon measures in these recipes are level, so skim off the excess with your finger or the blunt edge of a knife.

OVEN THERMOMETER

Baking requires accuracy, and as the internal thermostats of ovens vary, you may want to invest in an oven thermometer to make sure it is the correct temperature – and to identify any hotter or cooler spots.

PASTRY BRUSH

Available in a variety of widths and bristles. A medium-sized one with fine hair bristles is an ideal all-round one and is perfect for brushing on beaten egg, sugar syrup or melted butter. Choose one that is heat resistant and that can go in the dishwasher.

PIPING BAGS

Disposable plastic piping bags are widely available in various sizes and you can either snip off just the tip for piping icing and more delicate work, or cut a larger hole and use a piping nozzle. Large, seamless **nylon** piping bags are usually a little stronger and so are more useful for piping biscuits and choux pastry. They can be washed in hot soapy water and re-used but make sure they are completely dry inside and out before putting them away.

PIPING NOZZLES

These conical tubes fit in the end of piping bags and come in many shapes and sizes, from fine writing tips for icing lines to large star nozzles for piping biscuit dough. The best value sets are those that include a re-usable bag and a set of both large and small nozzles.

PUDDING BASINS AND MOULDS

Pudding basins come in a wide range of sizes and can be ceramic, glass or plastic. The best ones to use for steamed puddings are ceramic ones with a ridge around the top, which is essential for holding the string that seals the baking paper and foil in place, and for supporting the string handle that is used to lift the pudding out of the water or steamer, in recipes such as Christmas Pudding and Steamed Maple Syrup and Pecan Pudding (pages 74 and 64). For individual puddings, small pudding moulds are widely available; these are usually made from metal and are shaped like mini pudding basins. Dariole moulds are shaped like small flowerpots with straight sides, and are used in much the same way as the small pudding moulds. Either can be used in recipes as long as the volume of mixture that they hold is the same.

ROLLING PIN

A long wooden rolling pin is the best to get, as it allows you to roll out a large quantity of dough in a smooth, even layer. Don't leave it to soak in washing-up water, wipe it clean with a damp cloth after using and dry it well before putting it away, and never put it in the dishwasher or the wood will dry out and start to crack.

SCALES

Baking is a science and as accurate measurements are essential, a set of kitchen scales is a must. **Digital** scales are the most precise, especially when it comes to weighing out small quantities and so are preferable to **spring** or **balance** scales. They can measure weights as small as 1g and on some you can convert from grams to millilitres at the push of a button so you can add both solids and liquids to your mixing bowl. A helpful tip: always keep a spare battery in your kitchen drawer.

SIEVE

A fine-mesh sieve is essential for removing lumps from cocoa powder and icing sugar, and also helps to evenly combine flour with raising agents and spices when adding to a mix, as well as bringing air into the mixture. A large metal one is the most useful for dry ingredients as well as for pushing fruit through to remove pips. A small one is also handy for dusting finished bakes with icing sugar or cocoa powder.

SPATULA

A good-quality flexible rubber spatula is great for mixing ingredients together, scraping out bowls and spreading out mixtures. It can also be used to **fold in** instead of a large metal spoon.

STEAMER

A steamer is a two-tiered pan, where the top pan fits snugly inside the bottom one and the base is perforated with lots of holes to allow the steam to pass through. The lid should be a tight-fitting one to prevent too much steam escaping as your pudding cooks. Steamers can also be used for general cooking and so, although not an essential piece of kit, it is a versatile one. If you don't have a steamer you can improvise by putting a trivet or upturned saucer in the bottom of a deep pan and adding enough water to come half-way up the side of your pudding basin. Take care not to overfill the pan as you don't want the water bubbling into the pudding as it simmers.

THERMOMETER

This is an essential piece of kit to test the temperature of sugar syrups and jams, as the temperature reached greatly affects how they will perform. You can buy a sugar thermometer, which as well as the temperature gauge usually features a chart telling you which setting points are at which temperatures. A slightly more expensive but more versatile option is a digital thermometer, which has a metal probe and an LED display.

TIMER

It's very easy to get distracted once your bake has gone in the oven, so get in the habit of always setting a timer. Ideally, get one with seconds as well as minutes, and a long, loud ring. Set the timer for a bit less than the stated cooking time, as you can always cook it for longer if need be.

WHISKS AND MIXERS

These range from the most basic hand-held whisk, where you do all the work, through to free-standing mixers that do all the work for you.

Wire whisks can be balloon shaped or flat, and can be used for whisking mixtures and sauces both on and off the heat. Choose a sturdy one that fits your hand comfortably.

Rotary whisks have two beaters within a metal frame that are turned by hand. They are slightly more efficient than a wire whisk and so are good for whisking cream and egg whites and also for whisking mixtures on the hob as you don't have any trailing wires to contend with.

Hand-held electric mixers are much more powerful, but also more expensive. They are great though for creamed cake mixtures and meringues where a lot of whisking is involved, and they are more versatile and less expensive than a free-standing mixer as they can whisk over heat. Look for models with a set of attachments and a retractable cord for easy storage.

Free-standing electric mixers, although expensive, can save you a lot of time and energy if you are going to do a lot of baking. Most free-standing mixers come with three attachments: a paddle for creaming butter and sugar; a whisk for whisked sponges and meringues; and a dough hook for kneading dough, so they really are very versatile.

WOODEN SPOONS

Wooden spoons are heat resistant, won't scratch non-stick pans and are ideal for beating mixtures and stirring sauces. They come in all shapes and sizes and you can never have enough. The handles are also used for shaping biscuits such as the Brandy Snaps (page 132). Try to keep those used for baking separate from those used for frying or stirring savoury foods as they can absorb strong flavours.

ZESTER

The zest from oranges, lemons and limes is used a great deal in puddings and desserts. A long zester with a sturdy handle is better than a standard grater as it will grate just the zest without taking any of the bitter white pith with it.

Skills

Now that you have all your equipment and ingredients ready you can get baking. The recipes that follow are designed to take you step by step through all the skills you need to make delicious puddings and desserts, from an easy fruit crumble through to a showstopping millefeuilles. All the recipes tell you exactly what you need to do but you'll notice that some of the terms are highlighted in bold, which means you can refer back to this skills section if you want a bit more detail or you need a gentle reminder of any technique.

The following pages contain invaluable hints and tips from the experts to ensure you get great results every time you bake.

THE KEY TECHNIQUES FOR SPONGE CAKE, PASTRY AND MERINGUE

Because puddings and desserts can be so varied, you will find that you cover a wide range of baking skills as you work through the recipes in this book, but there are a few key techniques that will crop up time and again. Those key techniques are sponge cake, pastry and meringue. The two most common methods of making sponge are creamed sponge and whisked sponge, and both are explained below. This section will also explain everything you need to know to achieve the best results from the main types of pastries that are used in this book: shortcrust, pâte sucrée and puff. There are two types of meringue used in the recipes, French and Italian, both of which are made from egg whites and sugar.

CREAMED SPONGE

Butter, sugar, eggs and flour are combined to make a light sponge cake. Once you've mastered the basic sponge you can play around with flavours, but the technique is always the same. Make sure that all your ingredients are at room temperature as this ensures that they take in as much as air as possible, which is the key to achieving the right light texture.

1. Put the softened butter into a large bowl (or the bowl of a free-standing mixer) and beat with a wooden spoon or electric mixer until the butter is very creamy.

2. Gradually beat in the sugar, scraping down the sides of the bowl with a rubber spatula every now and then to ensure that all of the butter and sugar are combined. Keep beating and scraping until the mixture is pale in colour and has a light and fluffy texture (*see photo on page 23*).

3. Beat the eggs with a fork and then beat them into the mixture with a wooden spoon, a tablespoon at a time. Beat well between each addition to ensure that the egg is completely incorporated before you add the next bit. This thorough beating also adds air to the mixture, which will ensure that the baked sponge has a light texture. Add 1 tablespoon of the weighed flour from your recipe with each of the last two amounts of egg to prevent the mixture from curdling.

4. Sift the remaining flour into the bowl (plus any spices) and gently **fold** in with a large metal spoon, until the flour is mixed in fully and there are no clumps or streaks visible. You should have a nice soft mixture that just drops off your spoon.

5. Transfer the mixture to the prepared tin and bake immediately as the raising agents in the cake start to work straight away.

Learn with: Steamed Maple Syrup and Pecan Pudding (page 64), Orange Polenta Cake with Cranberry Sauce (page 66) and Sticky Toffee Pudding (page 68)

WHISKED SPONGE

The whisked method relies on the whisking of the eggs to make them light and fluffy rather than adding any raising agents. A genoise sponge, such as the Triple Chocolate Gateau (page 140) is a whisked sponge with the addition of a little melted butter added to the mix at the end (around 15g of butter per egg). This gives a richer and slightly softer sponge. 'Biscuit' sponges, like the sponge fingers in the Tiramisu Gateau (page 116) also use the whisked method, but the whites and yolks are whisked separately and then folded together. This creates a drier, more biscuit-like texture. The key to success with a whisked sponge is to to have a good

technique (see below) and to have the eggs at room temperature, as cold eggs don't expand as much on whisking. Ideally, you should use a hand-held electric whisk or a free-standing mixer fitted with a whisk attachment as a lot of whisking is required. If you don't have either you can still whisk by hand using a balloon whisk or rotary whisk but you'll need a lot of elbow grease, although the job can be made easier by placing the bowl over a pan of gently simmering water as the heat helps the eggs to expand. Don't let the bowl touch the water or the eggs may curdle.

How to make a simple whisked sponge
1. Whisk the eggs and sugar at high speed for about 5 minutes until they greatly increase in volume and are pale and creamy. The mixture should have a very thick mousse-like consistency and should pass the 'ribbon test'. To check this, lift the whisk out of the mixture and pass it across the bowl; it should leave a thick ribbon-like trail across the surface (*see photo, left*).
2. Sift the flour into the bowl and then very gently **fold** into the mixture. Make sure that you work quickly but gently as the light texture of the sponge relies on the air that you have whisked into the eggs.
Learn with: Peach Melba (page 70), Raspberry Trifle (page 108) and Baked Alaska (page 146)

SHORTCRUST PASTRY
Short pastries have a light and crumbly texture and need gentle handling. Kneading and handling develops and lengthens the gluten in the flour, which is an essential part of bread making but will give your pastry a tough consistency. You want the gluten to stay short so remember to handle it lightly. Shortcrust pastry is quick and easy to make

and so is ideal to start with. The traditional recipe uses half fat to flour and is a good rule to remember when you start to experiment with this pastry. It uses the rubbing-in method and can be made by hand or in a food-processor (see pages 32–33).

1. The butter must be well chilled for this pastry so use it straight from the fridge and cut it into cubes. Some recipes use other fats, but the recipes in this book use butter.

2. Rub the butter into the flour until you get a breadcrumb-like mix (*see photo, right*).

3. Add just enough cold water to form a dough; too much can result in tough pastry.

4. Shape the dough into a thick disc, wrap it in clingfilm and chill in the fridge for around 20 minutes until firm but not hard. Chilling will stop the pastry shrinking as it bakes.

5. Roll out the pastry and use it to **line** your tin or pie dish.

Learn with: Apple and Stem Ginger Lattice Tart (page 86)

RICH SHORTCRUST PASTRY

This is richer than regular shortcrust but it is made in much the same way, with the addition of egg yolks in place of some of the water and sometimes added butter. This gives the pastry a richer flavour and a slightly flakier texture. The protein in the egg yolk also makes the pastry more flexible so it is great for making tarts.

1. Follow the instructions for making shortcrust pastry but replace some of the water with egg yolk and add sugar to the flour if you are making a sweet dough.

2. Shape into a thick disc as before, wrap in clingfilm and chill in the fridge for around 20 minutes, then **roll out** and **line** your tin.

Learn with: Fig and Frangipane Tart (page 80)

PÂTE SUCRÉE

A rich buttery, sweet pastry that is made using softened butter and has more egg yolks and sugar than a rich shortcrust. It can also be made into a chocolate pastry with the addition of cocoa powder in place of some of the flour. It can crack easily as you roll it and can also become quite sticky so you might find it easier to roll it out between two sheets of baking paper as this will stop it from sticking to your work surface and enable you to turn the pastry easily.

1. Cream the softened butter and sugar with a wooden spoon until pale and soft in texture (*see photo, left*).

2. Mix in the egg yolks and flour with a little water until the mixture starts to come together.

3. Tip the dough onto a lightly floured work surface and gently knead it a few times until smooth. Shape into a disc, wrap in clingfilm and chill for 30–45 minutes until firm.

4. Roll out the pastry to the thickness of a £1 coin and use to **line** your flan tin.

Learn with: Chocolate and Orange Tarts with Cointreau Cream (page 96)

PUFF PASTRY

Puff pastry has a rich buttery taste and is crisp and light. The way it is made results in layers of fat and air being trapped between fine layers of dough which produces the rich and flaky layers. You can use plain or strong bread flour but the extra gluten in bread flour makes the dough stronger and more elastic and so gives the pastry extra lift in the layers. The pastry is also handled a lot and so the extra gluten helps it withstand that process. The addition of a little lemon juice helps it to keep its rich yellow colour.

1. Rub a small amount of butter into the flour and salt.

2. Form a fairly soft dough with cold water and a little lemon juice.

3. Knead the dough on a lightly floured surface for a few minutes to start to develop the gluten, then put it in a bowl, cover it with clingfilm and chill for 30 minutes.

4. Put the butter between two sheets of baking paper and using a rolling pin shape it into a square about 10cm across and 1cm thick, then chill with the dough.

5. On a lightly floured surface **roll** out the chilled dough into a square of about 20cm.

6. Peel the top layer of baking paper off the butter and upturn it into the centre of the dough so that the corners of the butter point at the middle of the sides of the dough. Fold each of the corners of the dough over the butter so that they meet in the middle and encase the butter (*see photo, top right*).

7. Give the dough a quarter turn so that a straight edge of the square is facing you. Make three indents in the dough with your rolling pin across the top, middle and bottom – this will squash the butter a bit and make sure that it forms an even layer as you roll out the dough. Roll the dough into a rectangle about 45 x 15cm.

8. Fold the bottom third up over the dough and the top third down to create a rectangle made up of three layers, brushing off any excess flour from the pastry as you fold (*see photo, bottom right*). Give the dough another quarter turn and repeat the rolling and folding process. Wrap the pastry in clingfilm and chill in the fridge for 30 minutes.

9. Repeat the above rolling, folding and chilling process twice more, so that in all you have rolled and folded the dough six times. Chill for 30 minutes before using.

Learn with: Pineapple Tarte Tatin (page 104) and Millefeuilles (page 150)

FRENCH MERINGUE

This is the most frequently used method of making meringue. It can be made in a bowl with a hand-held electric mixer or in a free-standing mixer using the whisk attachment. Make sure that your bowl and whisk are completely clean and dry, as any grease or water will stop your egg whites from stiffening. To ensure your bowl is as grease-free as possible rub the cut edge of a lemon around the inside before you add the egg whites. The trick is to add the sugar at the right stage. The eggs should be at soft peak stage; if you add the sugar too early it will dissolve and make the mixture soft and damp, but if the egg whites are too stiff the structure won't be elastic enough and will result in a lumpy meringue. Make sure the eggs are at room temperature before you start so they can achieve maximum volume.

1. Put the egg whites in a large bowl and whisk until they form **soft peaks**, do not over whisk at this stage or the egg whites will turn to liquid again.

2. Add the sugar gradually, a spoonful at a time and whisk well between each addition to ensure the sugar is fully whisked in before adding more, otherwise the meringue will have a grainy texture.

3. Continue whisking until all the sugar is added and the meringue is firm, glossy and has reached the **stiff peak** stage (*see photo, left*). The meringue is now ready to be piped or shaped and baked.

Learn with: Queen of Puddings (page 82), Tropical Pavlova (page 88) and Hazelnut Meringue Gateau (page 128)

ITALIAN MERINGUE

This meringue is made with boiling sugar syrup instead of caster sugar, which creates a much more stable meringue than French meringue. The hot syrup 'cooks' the egg whites so it is safe to use with either no further or very short baking. It creates a thick glossy meringue that holds it shape well as it cooks. As with French meringue, make sure that your bowl and whisk are completely clean and dry, as any grease or water will stop your egg whites from stiffening.

1. Put the sugar and a little water into a pan and heat over a gentle heat until the sugar has dissolved, swirl the pan gently to help the sugar dissolve rather than stir as this will stop sugar going up the sides of the pan which could develop into sugar crystals as the syrup boils.

2. Once you have a clear liquid increase the heat and bring the syrup to a boil (*see photo, right*). Put a kitchen thermometer into the liquid and simmer until the temperature reaches 120°C (250°F).

3. While the syrup cooks put the egg whites in a large heatproof bowl or the bowl of a free-standing mixer and whisk until they form **soft peaks**.

4. As soon as the syrup has reached the correct temperature remove it from the heat and pour in a thin, steady stream onto the whisked egg whites. Continue to whisk the whole time as you pour, taking care not to pour the syrup onto the whisk as it could splash and burn you.

5. Once all the syrup has been added carry on whisking until the meringue is smooth and glossy, has formed **stiff peaks** and is cool to the touch. Scrape the sides of the bowl with a spatula occasionally to ensure all of the egg white is fully whisked.

6. Pipe or shape the meringue and bake.
Learn with: Baked Alaska (page 146)

EXPERT ADVICE FROM START TO FINISH

This section will take you through everything you need to know to bake the recipes in this book, explaining the how, what and why behind the techniques to give you a full understanding.

HOW TO LINE CAKE TINS AND BAKING SHEETS

Most recipes ask you to line your cake tin or baking sheet. This will involve greasing it (usually with butter) and then lining either all or part of it with non-stick baking paper. This will stop your bake from sticking.

How to base line a cake tin

This is where just the base of the tin is lined with non-stick baking paper and the sides are greased. Put the tin on a sheet of non-stick baking paper and draw around the outside edge. Cut out the shape, then lightly brush melted butter inside the whole of the tin. Place the cut-out baking paper in the base of the tin and smooth down so that there are no creases.

How to line the sides of a cake tin

Cut out a piece of non-stick baking paper for the base as above, and also cut a strip that is long enough to cover the inside of the tin, and about 5cm taller than the tin. Make a fold along one long edge of the strip about 3cm deep, and snip all along the folded edge to the crease at about 1cm intervals. Brush the inside of the tin with melted butter, as above, then press the strip of baking paper inside the tin with the crease against the bottom edge so that the snipped edge sits on the bottom of the tin (*see photo, left*). Lightly butter the cut-out disc for the base, press on top and smooth down.

How to line a baking sheet

Tear off a sheet of non-stick baking paper the same size as your baking sheet. For mixtures that need spreading or piping it is good to hold the baking paper in place. You can do this by putting a small blob of the mixture on the baking sheet at each corner to stick the paper down.

HOW TO WHISK

Many of the recipes included in this book have a whisked element, be it egg whites for meringues or whole eggs and sugar for whisked sponges. Whisking incorporates air into a mixture and creates a light batter, which holds its structure when cooked.

How to whisk egg whites

You will need a large, spotlessly clean and grease-free mixing bowl; any trace of fat on the bowl or whisk will stop the egg whites from whisking properly, so to ensure your bowl is as grease-free as possible rub the cut edge of a lemon around the inside before you add the egg whites. Make sure the eggs are at room temperature before you start.

Put the egg whites in the bowl and whisk slowly until they turn frothy. A pinch of cream of tartar or lemon juice added now will help the structure to stiffen. Increase the speed and continue to whisk until the mixture has a fine, smooth texture. To test if the egg whites have reached **soft peak** stage, lift the whisk out: there should be a peak on the end that droops down slightly (*see photo, top right*). To get to **stiff peak** stage continue whisking. When you take the whisk out the peak should stand up in a stiff peak (*see photo, bottom right*) and you should also be able to turn the bowl upside down without the whites falling out.

HOW TO FOLD IN

Folding in lets you gently combine two or more ingredients without knocking any air out, such as adding flour to a creamed cake mix or egg whites to a cake batter, although it is a technique that is used in many other puddings and desserts, such as incorporating dates into Sticky Toffee Pudding (see page 68) and folding the crème pâtissière into the whipped cream for the Profiteroles with Salted Caramel and Chocolate Sauce (see page 124). Use the edge of a large metal spoon or plastic spatula and make a clean cut down the centre of the mix, making sure you touch the bottom of the bowl. Turn the spoon the right way up, scooping that half of the mixture up with you and gently pile it on top of the rest of the contents of the bowl (*see photo, top left*). Turn the bowl slightly so that you start in a different place and repeat the cutting, lifting and folding until all the ingredients are fully incorporated, using as few movements as possible.

HOW TO RUB IN

This is one of the most basic methods used in baking, especially in pastry-making but also for things like crumbles and cobblers. It refers to the way that the fat is rubbed into the flour using your fingertips, or a food-processor. It also adds air to the mixture, which gives a lighter finish to your bake. The key thing to remember is to keep everything, including your hands, as cold as possible, so use butter straight from the fridge.

How to rub in by hand

1. Put the flour and any other dry ingredients, such as salt, sugar or cocoa powder, into a large mixing bowl. There's no need to sift. Add the chilled diced butter.

2. Coat the cubes of butter in the flour mixture, using either your fingertips or a round-bladed knife. This will stop the cubes from sticking together as you start to work. **3.** Lift some of the butter and flour in your fingertips out of the bowl, allowing it to fall back into the bowl while gently rubbing your thumbs against the tips of your fingers to break the butter down into smaller pieces. **4.** Repeat this process, lifting your fingers well above the bowl each time to help to aerate the mixture, until it looks like fine breadcrumbs (*see photo on page 32, bottom*). If you shake the bowl any larger pieces will come to the surface.

How to rub in using a food-processor
1. Put your flour and any other dry ingredients into the bowl of the food-processor fitted with the metal blade. Add the chilled diced butter and pulse in short, sharp bursts until it looks like fine breadcrumbs. Be careful not to overwork the mixture or it could start to stick together before you add any liquid.

ROLLING OUT PASTRY
There are two key things to be aware of when rolling out pastry. The first is that your pastry is the correct consistency: it should be firm but not hard. If it's been in the fridge for a while, then leave it at room temperature for about 15 minutes to soften slightly so that it is easier to roll. If you try to roll it out when it is too firm you will have to press down harder with the rolling pin, which could result in a tough pastry. The second is to use the right amount of flour on your work surface: too much and it will add flour to the pastry, causing it to dry out; too little and the pastry may stick.

How to roll out pastry
1. Lightly dust the work surface with flour, smoothing it lightly with the palm of your hand so that you get an even layer. Put your dough onto the flour and move it around a little to coat the bottom in the flour.
2. Flatten the dough with your rolling pin and then start to roll from the edge nearest to you, pushing the rolling pin away from you in short, sharp movements. By rolling gently and in one direction the pastry is less likely to shrink as it bakes.
3. Give the pastry a quarter turn and roll again, keeping it in the shape of the tin you are going to line, so a circle for a round tin, etc. Keep the rolling pin lightly floured too so that the pastry doesn't stick to it. Wipe off any bits straight away, or they will make little dents in your pastry.
4. Don't turn your dough over, but roll it out on one side only (if it's turned over it will pick up more flour, and start drying and cracking). Turning the pastry regularly ensures it doesn't stick but if it does start to stick, drape it over your rolling pin to lift it off the work surface and sprinkle a little more flour underneath.
5. Check that the pastry is large enough to fit your tin or dish and that it is the correct thickness. A £1 coin is a good guide.

HOW TO LINE A TIN
Whether you're lining a large flan tin or dish, or smaller individual tins, your pastry needs to fit snugly, with no air pockets for it to shrink back into when it bakes.
1. Roll out your pastry to the correct size and thickness (see above) and drape it over your rolling pin. Try to have the rolling pin in the centre of the pastry so that the weight is evenly balanced as this will help prevent it from tearing.

33

2. Lift it up and gently lay it over the tin or dish, making sure that it is central and covers all sides (*see photo, top left*).

3. Remove the rolling pin and, working around the tin or dish, lift up a little of the pastry at a time and lower it down again, easing it into the inside edge. Make sure there are no air pockets in the side or on the bottom, and that the pastry sits right against the base and edges.

4. Gently press the pastry against the inside edge all the way round, either using your fingertips or a small ball of pastry. Some recipes will now ask you to trim off the excess pastry either using a small sharp knife, pressing the side of the knife against the tin to make sure you get a neat edge, or by rolling the rolling pin over the top of the tin – the sharp edges of the tin will cut through the overhanging pastry.

5. If you are lining a fluted flan tin, use the edge of your finger to press the pastry into the flutes to make sure it is lining the tin snugly (*see photo, bottom left*).

HOW TO BLIND BAKE

This is where the pastry case is first baked before you add the filling to prevent the pastry becoming soggy on the bottom, particularly with tarts with a runny filling.

1. Once you've lined your tin with pastry, lightly prick the base with a fork. Don't push the prongs of the fork right through the pastry or your filling might leak through the holes. Chill the pastry in its tin in the fridge.

2. Take a piece of baking paper larger than your flan tin and crumple it slightly in your hands. Lay it on top of the pastry and gently push it into the edges.

3. Tip in some baking beans (or uncooked rice) and spread out to form a layer that covers the whole of the base, ensuring they

go right to the edges as this will help the pastry keep its shape (*see photo, top right*).
4. Bake the pastry for the time specified in the recipe, which will cause it to firm up and hold its shape. Carefully remove the baking paper and beans – they will be hot so hold the paper on both sides so the beans don't tip out as you lift.
5. Put the pastry case back in the oven and bake again to finish cooking. The base and sides should be cooked through and pale and golden. If your tart is going to have a cold filling (i.e. it won't be going back in the oven), you can make extra sure it's fully cooked by baking it to a slightly deeper colour. Remove from the oven and leave to cool before adding any filling.

HOW TO MELT CHOCOLATE
Low and slow are the key points to remember. If you overheat or scorch it, it will 'seize', which means it becomes greasy and grainy and can't be used. White chocolate and dark chocolate with a high cocoa solid content (over 70 per cent) are most prone to seizing. Although you can melt chocolate in a microwave it is easier to control the temperature if you melt it in a bowl over a pan of simmering water.
1. Finely chop your chocolate as this will help it to melt evenly, then put it into a heatproof bowl that fits snugly over a pan of gently simmering water. Make sure the bottom of the bowl doesn't touch the water below or the chocolate could overheat.
2. Leave the chocolate to melt from the heat of the water for a couple of minutes before giving it a gentle stir with a spoon until it's completely glossy and smooth (*see photo, bottom right*). As soon as it's all melted remove from the pan so that it doesn't continue heating.

HOW TO WHIP CREAM

Whipped cream appears in several of the recipes in this book, whether folded into a cream cheese mixture for the Key Lime Cheesecake (see page 60) or sweetened with icing sugar to create the filling for the Tropical Pavlova (see page 88). Double cream and whipping cream are both suitable for whipping; whichever you use make sure it is thoroughly chilled before you start to prevent it from curdling. Use a hand-held wire whisk (a large balloon one is best), hand-held rotary whisk, electric whisk or free-standing mixer. If the cream is going to be folded into another mixture or used to top pudding such as the Raspberry Trifle (see page 108), then whisk it on a medium speed to a **soft peak** stage. Reduce the speed as it starts to thicken as it can be easily over-whipped. If the cream is going to be piped or folded into a crème pâtissière, then whisk it for a few more seconds until it forms **stiff peaks** (*see photo, left*).

HOW TO USE A PIPING BAG

Many of the recipes in this book include piping, whether it is a biscuit mix for the fingers in Tiramisu, a filling for the Triple Chocolate Gateau or putting the finishing touches to a dessert such as the Hazelnut Meringue Gateau (see pages 116, 140 or 128). Whichever recipe it is for the general piping techniques apply.

How to fill a piping bag

1. Drop the nozzle into the piping bag and pull it down so that it fits the hole tightly and there are no gaps, otherwise the filling will ooze out as you pipe. If you are using a disposable bag you will need to snip off the end to create the hole.

2. Put the bag into a tall jug or container and fold the top edge of the bag over the rim to support the bag.

3. Spoon the filling into the bag until it is about two-thirds full; if you overfill it it makes the bag difficult to handle and so to pipe. (*see photo, right*)

4. Take the bag out of the jug and twist the top to push out any air bubbles and then twist again to push the filling down into the nozzle.

How to pipe

A firm and steady hand is essential to ensure smooth and even piping, so hold the piping bag in both hands with your stronger hand at the top of the bag and your other hand at the bottom near the nozzle to help guide the bag. Squeeze the bag gently using even pressure so that the mix or icing comes out in a smooth flow.

If you are piping biscuits onto baking paper, ensure all the biscuits are even in length by drawing two parallel lines onto the paper first and then pipe between those lines. When piping rounds such as the macarons for the Trio of Tropical Desserts (see page 154), you can draw the circles first on the paper, again to ensure that you achieve consistent sizes.

Help!

No matter how experienced a baker you are, things can still go wrong. Here are some of the most common problems that you might come up against and some tips on how to put them right.

MY CREAMED CAKE MIXTURE HAS CURDLED!

There are several reasons why this might have happened, but it can be fixed. The most common reason is that either your butter or eggs were too cold. If the butter is too cold it won't be soft enough to cream properly when beaten with the sugar. If your eggs are too cold they again will be hard to beat into the butter and sugar and so the mixture may curdle.

Ideally, all ingredients should be at room temperature before you begin; if your butter is still too hard, then soften it slightly in the microwave, but go carefully you don't want to melt it. If you add the eggs too quickly to the creamed butter and sugar your mixture may curdle, so make sure you add them a little at a time and beat well between each addition. If the mix does start to curdle then add a tablespoon of flour and beat that in; this should help bring the mixture together again.

MY CREAM IS TOO STIFF!

This is an easy mistake to make when whipping cream: one minute it's soft and fluffy, the next it's standing in stiff peaks. The way to avoid this is to watch it very carefully and at the point when it starts to thicken start to whisk more slowly in short sharp bursts and keep regularly checking the consistency. If it does become too thick pour in a little un-whipped cream and lightly fold through to loosen the over-whipped cream.

MY PASTRY CASE HAS SHRUNK!

This can happen if the pastry has been over-handled and stretched when rolled; it then shrinks back during baking. To avoid this, roll out your pastry gently and in one direction at a time, then ease it into the tin, pushing the pastry down from the top edge to fit into the sides of the tin rather than stretching it over. Chilling the pastry case before baking allows the pastry to relax again after handling and so should stop it from shrinking.

If your pastry case does still shrink it's not the end of the world; you just might not be able to use all of the filling. If the filling spills over the top edge it might cause the pastry case to stick to the tin and you'll have trouble getting it out to serve.

MY BISCUITS AREN'T BAKING EVENLY!

Most ovens don't bake entirely evenly throughout and have hot spots, so to ensure your biscuits bake evenly turn the baking sheets round halfway through baking. If you are baking a large batch of biscuits on more than one sheet, then you can also swap shelves at the same time. Using the fan setting on your oven helps to circulate the heat and so should give a more even bake. It is also a good idea to invest in an oven thermometer so you can make sure your oven is reaching the correct temperature and to identify the hotter and cooler spots.

MY CUSTARD HAS CURDLED!

If you cook your custard for too long or over too high a heat there is a chance that the eggs will overcook and curdle – almost like scrambled eggs in hot cream. To avoid this, don't let the mixture get too hot and keep stirring it. If it does split, plunge the pan into a bowl or sink of cold water so that the water comes up the side of the pan to cool it. Then whisk vigorously, preferably using a balloon whisk; this should break up the curdled eggs and bring the custard back together again.

....

MY CHOCOLATE IS GRAINY!

If your chocolate is overheated or comes into contact with any water while it melts it might well turn thick and grainy (this is known as 'seizing') rather than melting to a smooth and glossy consistency. So when melting chocolate over a pan of water ensure that the water is simmering gently and not boiling and that the bottom of the bowl doesn't touch the water as that is when it is most likely to overheat. You should also make sure that the bowl fits snugly over the pan as if there is a large gap steam could get through the gap and might well get into the chocolate. When melting chocolate in a microwave, set the heat to the lowest setting possible and melt the chocolate in short sharp bursts, stirring well in between to ensure that no hot spots form, which could then seize.

Before you throw away any seized chocolate it is worth trying to rescue it; this can be done in one of two ways. Remove the bowl of chocolate from the heat and beat in either a little vegetable oil or – strange as it might seem – a little boiling water. Add just a teaspoonful at a time and beat well between each addition. With a little bit of luck it will come back to a smooth, glossy consistency.

....

MY PUFF PASTRY DIDN'T PUFF UP!

It is the butter trapped between the layers of puff pastry that makes it puff up, so to ensure the butter stays in the layers it must be chilled at all times. If the butter is allowed to soften too much as you roll out the pastry it will slide out from between the layers. It is important to chill the pastry thoroughly between each of the folding and rolling stages. If at any point you think it has become too warm, simply pop it in the freezer for 10–15 minutes.

When baking puff pastry make sure the oven is hot enough when the pastry first goes in to ensure the layers puff up. As soon as the pastry goes into a hot oven, the butter produces steam, which is what causes the layers to rise.

BAKE IT
BETTER
Recipes

Apple Strudel

Layers of crisp filo pastry encase apple, sultanas and cinnamon to create this great teatime classic, lightly dusted with icing sugar.

1 cooking apple
75g soft light brown sugar
1 teaspoon ground cinnamon
50g unsalted butter
4 sheets of bought filo pastry
50g sultanas
icing sugar, for dusting

HANDS-ON TIME:
20 minutes

BAKING TIME:
30–35 minutes

SERVES:
8

SPECIAL
EQUIPMENT:
large baking sheet

1. Preheat the oven to 180°C (160°C fan), 350°F, Gas 4 and **line** the baking sheet with a piece of baking paper.

2. Peel, core and thinly slice the apple and place the slices in a bowl. Sprinkle over the sugar and cinnamon, and stir to coat the slices.

3. Melt the butter in a small pan. Take a sheet of filo pastry and lay it on your work surface with the short edge towards you. Use a pastry brush to brush all over the pastry with butter and lay another sheet on top. Brush this with butter and repeat the brushing and layering with the last two sheets of pastry.

4. Place the apple slices in an even layer on the front half of the pastry sheets, then sprinkle over the sultanas. Starting at the front edge, roll up the pastry to fully encase the filling. Using two metal spatulas, carefully transfer the strudel to the lined baking sheet and brush all over with the remaining melted butter. Bake in the oven for 30–35 minutes until crisp and golden.

5. Leave to cool for 10 minutes on the baking sheet before carefully transferring to a wire rack and leaving to cool completely. Dust with icing sugar and serve cut into thick slices.

Try Something Different

Replace the cinnamon with 1 teaspoon of grated orange zest, and the sultanas with cranberries.

Coconut and Lime Rice Pudding

A great pudding to get you started, rich and creamy oven-baked rice pudding with the addition of lime zest to add extra flavour and served with a pretty raspberry sauce.

HANDS-ON TIME:
10 minutes

BAKING TIME:
1½–1¾ hours

SERVES:
4–6

SPECIAL
EQUIPMENT:
heavy-based
flameproof casserole
dish, about
1.5–2 litre capacity

For the rice pudding

25g unsalted butter
100g pudding rice
60g caster sugar
400ml full-fat milk
1 × 400ml tin coconut milk
finely grated zest of 2 limes

For the raspberry sauce

150g fresh or frozen raspberries
(you can use frozen raspberries
straight from the freezer)
50g caster sugar
juice of 1 lime

1. Preheat the oven to 140°C (120°C fan), 275°F, Gas 1.

2. To make the rice pudding, put the butter in the casserole dish and place it over a medium heat to melt. Tip in the rice and stir to coat the grains in the butter, then add the sugar and stir again for about 5 minutes, until the sugar melts and the rice becomes sticky.

3. Pour in both the full-fat and coconut milk, stirring as you add them to stop any lumps forming. Bring the rice mixture to a simmer, then remove from the heat and stir in the lime zest.

4. Cover the dish with foil and bake in the oven for 1½ hours, giving it a stir every half an hour. Covering it will prevent it from browning.

5. When the pudding is done it will be thick and creamy and the grains will be soft and tender. If you want to be sure that the rice is cooked through, carefully scoop out a few grains from the edge to check. If the rice still has some bite and all the milk hasn't been absorbed, give it a stir and return it to the oven for a further 10–15 minutes. Remove from the oven and leave to rest for 10–15 minutes before serving.

6. While the pudding rests, make the raspberry sauce. Put the raspberries, caster sugar and lime juice in a small pan and heat for 4–5 minutes over a low heat until the sugar has dissolved and the raspberries just start to soften. Serve the rice pudding topped with the raspberry sauce.

Try Something Different

Replace the coconut milk with double cream and the lime zest with lemon zest for a more traditionally flavoured pudding.

Orange and Cranberry Bread and Butter Pudding

Layers of fruit bread, orange zest and cranberries baked in a rich creamy custard make this a zesty update of an all-time favourite pudding. Take time to overlap the bread slices in neat rows to show the pudding at its best.

10 slices fruit bread
50g unsalted butter, softened, plus extra for greasing
100g dried cranberries
finely grated zest of 1 orange
4 medium eggs
300ml full-fat milk
300ml double cream
100g golden caster sugar

Easy does it

HANDS-ON TIME:
20 minutes

HANDS-OFF TIME:
1 hour

BAKING TIME:
45 minutes

SERVES:
6

SPECIAL EQUIPMENT:
20 × 25cm shallow baking dish

1. Butter each slice of fruit bread and cut each slice in half to create two triangles, so that you have 20 triangles in total. Butter the baking dish.

2. In a small bowl mix the cranberries with the orange zest so that the cranberries are coated; this will help to make sure that the zest is spread throughout the pudding. Crack the eggs into a large jug and beat lightly with a fork. Add the milk, double cream and sugar and beat again to combine.

3. Put half the bread triangles in the base of the baking dish, overlapping each piece slightly. Scatter half the cranberry and orange mix over the slices, then top with the rest of the bread, overlapping the slices as before. Scatter over the remaining cranberries. Give the egg and milk mixture a final whisk with the fork to stop the sugar from sinking to the bottom. Pour over the bread and fruit, making sure that you coat all the bread slices with the liquid to prevent any dry patches of pudding. Put to one side for 1 hour to let the bread soak up the custard, and gently push down any corners of bread on the top layer that are poking out as it rests.

4. Preheat the oven to 180°C (160°C fan), 350°F, Gas 4. Bake the pudding for 45 minutes until the top is crisp and golden. Leave to rest for 15 minutes before serving either on its own or with a drizzle of extra cream.

Try Something Different

Replace the cranberries with sultanas and use lemon zest instead of orange. You could also use slices of brioche in place of the fruit bread.

Spiced Plum Crumble

A crumble topping is a great way to learn the rubbing-in technique used in pastry-making. Cinnamon and mixed spice are a perfect combination with plums in this crumble filling.

For the fruity filling
800g plums
75g soft light brown sugar
1 teaspoon ground cinnamon
1 teaspoon mixed spice

For the crumble topping
200g plain flour
100g chilled unsalted butter, diced
75g porridge oats
125g soft light brown sugar

1. Preheat the oven to 190°C (170°C fan), 375°F, Gas 5.

2. For the filling, cut the plums in half around the stone and twist the two halves apart. Remove the stones and cut each piece in half again so you end up with quarters. Put all the plum pieces into a bowl, then sprinkle over the sugar and spices, stir to coat the plums, then tip them into the base of the baking dish.

3. To make the crumble topping, put the flour in a bowl and add the butter. **Rub in** the butter to make coarse crumbs, then stir in the oats and sugar.

4. Scatter the crumble topping over the plums, covering them in an even layer. Don't pat the topping down; just let it sit on top of the fruit as this will give a crisper topping.

5. Bake in the oven for 40–45 minutes, or until the topping is golden and you can see the plum juices bubbling up the sides. Serve warm with custard or ice cream.

Try Something Different

Replace some of the plums with 100g blackberries when in season for a juicy alternative, and swap porridge oats for chopped toasted hazelnuts to add crunch to the topping.

Easy does it

HANDS-ON TIME:
15 minutes

BAKING TIME:
40–45 minutes

SERVES:
6

SPECIAL EQUIPMENT:
shallow baking dish, about 1.5 litre capacity

Cherry Clafoutis

Fresh cherries are marinated in sugar and kirsch then covered in a light batter and baked in the oven to make this classic French dessert.

HANDS-ON TIME:
15 minutes

HANDS-OFF TIME:
30 minutes

BAKING TIME:
30–35 minutes

SERVES:
6

SPECIAL EQUIPMENT:
25cm round, shallow baking dish, about 4cm deep

For the cherries
450g cherries
3 tablespoons caster sugar
3 tablespoons kirsch

For the batter
butter, for greasing
60g plain flour
½ teaspoon baking powder
60g caster sugar
3 medium eggs, lightly beaten
½ teaspoon vanilla extract
300ml full-fat milk
1 tablespoon icing sugar, for dusting

1. Butter a shallow baking dish that is wide enough to take the cherries in a single layer. You can check this by putting the cherries in the dish before you soak them.

2. Wash the cherries and remove any stalks, then remove the stones. A cherry pitter is best used for this as it takes out the stones but leaves the cherry whole. If you don't have one you can cut the cherries in half and take the stones out that way. Put the cherries in a bowl, add the sugar and kirsch, then stir gently to coat. Put to one side for 30 minutes to allow the cherries to absorb the flavour of the kirsch.

3. Preheat the oven to 180°C (160°C fan), 350°F, Gas 4.

4. To make the batter, sift the flour and baking powder into a mixing bowl and stir in the caster sugar. Pour the beaten eggs into the bowl and whisk into the flour until you have a smooth batter. Add the vanilla extract to the milk, then pour into the batter, whisking as you pour to make sure the batter stays smooth and you don't get any lumps.

5. Tip the cherries and any juices in the bowl into the baking dish and shake the dish to make sure the cherries are in a single layer. Pour the batter over the cherries. Bake in the oven for 30–35 minutes until golden on top and the clafoutis is just set but still a bit wobbly in the centre. Serve warm, dusted with icing sugar, and some cream.

Lemon and Blueberry Tart

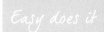

Easy does it

HANDS-ON TIME:
15 minutes

BAKING TIME:
15 minutes

SERVES:
6

SPECIAL
EQUIPMENT:
large baking sheet

A quick and easy dessert made using bought ready-rolled puff pastry. The pastry is baked first and then topped with creamy lemon and mascarpone cheese, and glossy fresh blueberries.

For the pastry base
1 × 375g sheet ready-rolled puff pastry
1 medium egg, lightly beaten

For the topping
50g caster sugar
finely grated zest and juice of 1 unwaxed lemon
250g fresh blueberries
250g mascarpone cheese
40g icing sugar
100ml double cream

1. Preheat the oven to 200°C (180°C fan), 400°F, Gas 6. Take the pastry out of the fridge 10–15 minutes before you use it – this will stop it from cracking when you unroll it.

2. **Line** the baking sheet with baking paper. Unroll the pastry onto the baking sheet and, using a small sharp knife, score a line around the sides of the pastry 1.5cm in from the edges, to create a border. Use a fork to prick all over the centre of the pastry rectangle to stop it rising too much during cooking. Brush the border with the beaten egg.

3. Bake in the oven for 15–20 minutes until risen and golden. Remove and leave to cool on the baking sheet for 5 minutes, then gently push the centre of the pastry down with your fingertips to flatten it and make room for the filling. Carefully lift the pastry off the baking paper and transfer to a wire rack to cool completely.

4. For the topping, put the caster sugar and 1 tablespoon of the lemon juice in a small pan and heat gently over a low heat until the sugar has dissolved. Add the blueberries to the pan, turn up the heat slightly and cook the blueberries in the sugar syrup for 2 minutes until they are glossy. Put to one side to cool.

5. Put the mascarpone cheese into a mixing bowl and beat with a wooden spoon until smooth. Sift in the icing sugar, add the remainder of the lemon juice and the lemon zest and beat again. Finally, add the double cream and beat until thick and creamy.

6. Spread the mascarpone mixture on top of the pastry case right up to the raised edges or the border, smoothing the surface as you go. Scatter over the cooled blueberries and any juices left in the bowl. Serve immediately.

Try Something Different

Swap the blueberries for the same amount of strawberries (halved if large) but don't cook them in the sugar syrup as they will go mushy; just stir them into the warm syrup and allow to cool.

Rhubarb Cobbler

The rubbing-in technique is used here to make this cobbler. The topping is made with buttermilk to create a scone-like texture, which makes a tasty change from a rhubarb crumble.

For the filling
1kg rhubarb
2 teaspoons vanilla bean paste
150g caster sugar

For the cobbler topping
250g self-raising flour
100g chilled unsalted butter, diced
100g caster sugar
150ml buttermilk

Easy does it

HANDS-ON TIME:
15 minutes

BAKING TIME:
35–40 minutes

SERVES:
6

SPECIAL
EQUIPMENT:
22 × 30cm shallow
baking dish,
1.5 litre capacity

1. Preheat the oven to 180°C (160°C fan), 350°F, Gas 4.

2. For the filling, trim the ends from the rhubarb and then cut each stick into 4–5cm long pieces. Put these into a large bowl, add the vanilla bean paste and caster sugar and gently stir to coat the rhubarb in both. Tip into the baking dish and gently shake so that the rhubarb settles into an even layer.

3. For the cobbler topping, sift the flour into a mixing bowl and add the butter. **Rub in** the butter with your fingertips to make coarse crumbs, then stir in the caster sugar. Add the buttermilk and stir in with a wooden spoon until just mixed and you have a soft, wet dough.

4. Use a dessertspoon to drop dollops of the dough on top of the rhubarb, leaving small gaps in between each one to allow for them to spread as they cook. Bake in the oven for 35–40 minutes, or until the top is crisp and golden. Serve warm from the oven with a scoop of ice cream or a spoonful of cream.

Try Something Different

To add an extra flavour and crunch to the dish, scatter 30g flaked almonds over the cobbler topping before baking.

Lemon and Aniseed Surprise Pudding

This zesty pudding gives you a chance to try out both creaming and whisking skills in one easy bake that separates on cooking to leave a fluffy sponge on top of a lemony 'surprise' sauce.

175g caster sugar
1 teaspoon aniseeds
75g unsalted butter, softened, plus extra for greasing
3 medium eggs, at room temperature, separated
finely grated zest and juice of 2 unwaxed lemons
75g self-raising flour
400ml full-fat milk

Easy does it

HANDS-ON TIME:
20 minutes

BAKING TIME:
30–35 minutes

SERVES:
4

SPECIAL EQUIPMENT:
baking dish,
1.5 litre capacity

METHOD USED:
Creamed sponge,
pages 22–23

1. Preheat the oven to 180°C (160°C fan), 350°F, Gas 4 and lightly butter the baking dish.

2. Put 75g of the caster sugar and the aniseeds into the bowl of a mini food-processor and blitz to create a fine powder. (You could also do this by hand with a pestle and mortar; it will just take you a little longer.)

3. Cream the softened butter, aniseed sugar and the remaining caster sugar together in a bowl using a wooden spoon (or a hand-held electric mixer) until thoroughly combined and paler in colour; it won't cream to a light and fluffy texture as there is more sugar than butter in the mixture. Add the egg yolks, beating well between each one, then add the lemon zest and beat again.

4. Add half the lemon juice to the creamed mix and **fold** in, then add half the flour and fold that in too. Repeat with the remaining lemon juice and flour. Add the milk to the cake mixture 100ml at a time, folding in each measure as you go. Adding it slowly like this ensures you get a smooth batter.

5. In a separate bowl and using clean beaters for your hand-held electric mixer, **whisk** the egg whites to **soft peaks** (they should just hold their shape when you remove the whisk from the bowl). Fold these into the lemony batter until you have no big lumps of egg white remaining. It may curdle a bit at this stage, but that's perfectly normal and won't affect the texture of the sponge.

6. Pour the mixture into the baking dish. Bake in the oven for 30–35 minutes until well risen and golden on top. Leave for 10 minutes to allow the sauce to separate out from the pudding before serving warm.

Try Something Different

Leave out the aniseeds, omitting step 2 and adding all the caster sugar in step 3. Or replace the aniseeds with 1 teaspoon of dried lavender.

Individual Treacle Tarts

Try out your blind-baking skills with these easy-to-make tarts. Using bought shortcrust pastry and a very simple but classic filling means they can be baked in no time.

500g bought shortcrust pastry
250g golden syrup
100g fresh breadcrumbs
finely grated zest and juice of 1 unwaxed lemon

Easy does it

HANDS-ON TIME:
20 minutes

HANDS-OFF TIME:
20 minutes chilling

BAKING TIME:
35 minutes

MAKES:
6 tartlets

SPECIAL EQUIPMENT:
6 × 10cm loose-bottomed tart tins, baking sheet

1. Divide the pastry into six equal portions, then **roll out** each piece on a lightly floured surface into a circle about the thickness of a £1 coin. **Line** the tart tins, pressing the pastry into the edges with a small ball of the dough. Roll your rolling pin over the top of the tart tins to cut off any excess pastry and prick the bases with a fork. Place on a baking sheet and chill in the fridge for 15 minutes.

2. Preheat the oven to 200°C (180°C fan), 400°F, Gas 6. Line each pastry case with a small circle of baking paper and fill with a handful of baking beans or uncooked rice. **Blind bake** in the oven for 10 minutes, then remove the paper and beans, and bake for a further 5 minutes until the bases look cooked and are pale golden. Remove from the oven and lower the temperature to 180°C (160°C fan), 350°F, Gas 4.

3. Gently heat the golden syrup in a medium pan to melt it slightly. Remove from the heat and add the breadcrumbs, lemon zest and juice and stir to evenly coat the crumbs.

4. Divide the mixture between the six tart cases, flattening the top lightly with the back of a spoon. Bake in the oven for 20 minutes, until golden on top.

5. Leave to cool for 10 minutes in the tart tins, before removing from the tins. Serve warm with custard or a dollop of lightly whipped cream.

Try Something Different

Add extra crunch by replacing 25g of the breadcrumbs with 25g finely chopped pecans or walnuts.

Key Lime Cheesecake

A chilled cheesecake that is easy to assemble, with the minimum of baking. A chocolate crust is covered with a rich, creamy lime and cream cheese topping.

Easy does it

HANDS-ON TIME:
30 minutes

BAKING TIME:
10 minutes

SERVES:
12

SPECIAL
EQUIPMENT:
20cm springclip
cake tin

For the chocolate base
150g digestive biscuits
50g unsalted butter
40g dark chocolate, preferably 60–70 per cent cocoa solids, chopped

For the topping
3 sheets of leaf gelatine (see page 14)
100ml soured cream
300g cream cheese
150g golden caster sugar
finely grated zest and juice of 3 limes, plus zest of 1 lime for decorating
300ml double cream, well chilled

1. Preheat the oven to 180°C (160°C fan), 350°F, Gas 4. Butter the tin and **line** the base and sides with baking paper.

2. To make the chocolate base, put the digestive biscuits in a plastic food bag, seal the top, then bash with a rolling pin to create fine biscuit crumbs (you can whizz them in a food-processor, but bashing them is quick and easy and creates a lot less washing up). Gently **melt** the butter and chocolate in a heatproof bowl in the microwave, or in a heatproof bowl set over a pan of gently simmering water, making sure that the bottom of the bowl doesn't touch the water. Add the biscuit crumbs to the bowl and stir to coat.

3. Tip the biscuit mix into the tin and smooth down to cover the base; if you press it down using a potato masher it will help you get a nice even layer. Bake in the oven for 10 minutes, then put to one side to cool while you make the topping.

4. Soak the gelatine in a bowl of cold water for 10 minutes to soften. Meanwhile, heat the soured cream in a small pan until bubbling and remove from the heat. Lift the softened gelatine leaves from the cold water and squeeze gently to remove the excess water, then add to the warm soured cream and stir until they have all melted.

5. Put the cream cheese and caster sugar in a large mixing bowl and beat together with a wooden spoon until creamy and thoroughly combined. Add the lime zest and juice along with the cooled soured cream and gelatine mixture and beat again until smooth.

6. In a separate bowl, **whip** the double cream with a hand-held electric mixer to **soft peaks**, then **fold** into the cream cheese mix until fully combined. Pour over the cooled biscuit base and smooth the top with the back of a spoon. Put in the fridge to set for at least 3 hours.

7. Remove from the tin and peel off the baking paper from the sides. You can either serve this on the base or use a palette knife to slide the cheesecake onto a serving plate. Sprinkle the extra grated lime zest on the top.

Pear and Chocolate Upside-down Cake

Here, a light chocolatey sponge sits on top of gently caramelised pear slices. This is a good recipe to perfect the **creamed method** of cake making.

150g unsalted butter, softened, plus extra for greasing
150g soft light brown sugar, plus 2 tablespoons
3 medium eggs, at room temperature, lightly beaten
150g self-raising flour
50g cocoa powder
4 tablespoons full-fat milk
1 just-ripe pear

Easy does it

HANDS-ON TIME:
20 minutes

BAKING TIME:
30 minutes

SERVES:
10–12

SPECIAL EQUIPMENT:
20cm round cake tin, about 6cm deep

METHOD USED:
Creamed sponge, pages 22–23

1. Preheat the oven to 180°C (160°C fan), 350°F, Gas 4. Butter and **line** the base of the tin with baking paper. Sprinkle the 2 tablespoons of sugar in the base of the tin on top of the baking paper.

2. Cream together the softened butter and sugar in a mixing bowl with a wooden spoon until pale and fluffy (or use a hand-held electric mixer). Gradually add the eggs, a little at a time, beating well between each addition so that the mixture doesn't curdle. If it does curdle at any point, add a spoonful of the flour with the egg.

3. Sift the flour and cocoa powder into the bowl and **fold** in gently; when it's nearly all folded in add the milk and carry on folding until you have a cake mixture with a soft dropping consistency. This means that the mixture will drop from a spoon back into the bowl if you hold a full spoon of batter above the bowl. If the batter is still too stiff, then add a little extra milk.

4. Peel the pear and remove the stalk. Cut the pear into quarters and remove the cores, then cut each quarter into 3 slices to give you 12 slices in total. Lay the pear slices on top of the sugar in the cake tin in a circle with the thin tips of the pear in the middle to create a flower.

5. Carefully spoon the chocolate cake mixture on top of the pear slices, taking care not to move the slices, then smooth the top of the batter with the back of a spoon. Bake in the oven for about 30 minutes until the cake starts to come away from the sides of the tin and a skewer inserted into the centre comes out clean.

6. Leave to cool for about 5 minutes in the tin, then turn out onto a serving plate. Carefully peel off the baking paper to reveal the pear slices. Cut into slices and serve warm with softly whipped double cream or a scoop of vanilla ice cream.

Steamed Maple Syrup and Pecan Pudding

There is nothing more comforting than a classic sponge pudding, and this combination of maple syrup and pecan hits the spot. Here, the cake batter is steamed instead of baked.

125g unsalted butter, softened, plus extra for greasing
125g soft dark brown sugar
2 medium eggs, at room temperature, lightly beaten
175g self-raising flour
4 tablespoons maple syrup
75g pecans

Easy does it

HANDS-ON TIME:
20 minutes

STEAMING TIME:
1½ hours

SERVES:
6

SPECIAL EQUIPMENT:
1 litre pudding basin

METHOD USED:
Creamed sponge,
pages 22–23

1. Liberally butter the pudding basin and **line** the base with a circle of baking paper. Draw around the top of the basin and cut out a baking paper circle for the top. Place a trivet or upturned saucer in the bottom of a large pan so that the basin isn't over the direct heat and add enough water to come halfway up the sides of the pudding basin.

2. Cream together the butter and sugar in a bowl with a wooden spoon (or use a free-standing mixer) until pale and creamy. Add the eggs one at a time, beating well after each addition. **Fold** in the flour and half the maple syrup.

3. Arrange 9 pecans in the base of the pudding basin, their tops facing down. Pour over the remaining maple syrup. Roughly chop the rest of the pecans and fold them into the sponge mixture.

4. Carefully spoon the mixture into the pudding basin on top of the pecans. Use the back of a spoon to smooth the surface and place the circle of baking paper on top. Take a large square of foil and fold a pleat down the centre to allow room for the pudding to rise.

Place this on top of the basin and press down around the edge. Tie a piece of string around the basin, under the rim. Take another piece of string and create a handle by passing it under the tied string on both sides of the basin (see step photos on pages 76–77). Bring the pan of water to the boil.

5. Place the basin in the pan on top of the trivet or saucer and cover with a tight-fitting lid. Steam for 1½ hours, topping up the pan with boiled water when needed to prevent it boiling dry.

6. To serve, run a knife around the inside of the basin to loosen the pudding. Put a plate on top of the basin and, using a tea towel wrapped around the basin, turn the pudding out onto the plate. Remove the circle of baking paper and serve with custard or cream.

Try Something Different

To make a chocolate pudding, mix 4 tablespoons cocoa powder with 1 tablespoon hot water. Fold in with the flour instead of the syrup and nuts.

Orange Polenta Cake with Cranberry Sauce

The polenta adds a great crunch to this moist gluten-free sponge, flavoured with orange, topped with a sugar syrup and served with a tangy cranberry sauce.

HANDS-ON TIME:
30 minutes

BAKING TIME:
1 hour

SERVES:
12

SPECIAL
EQUIPMENT:
20cm springclip
cake tin

METHOD USED:
Creamed sponge,
pages 22–23

For the cake

225g unsalted butter, softened, plus extra for greasing
225g caster sugar
4 medium eggs, at room temperature, lightly beaten
1 teaspoon vanilla extract
finely grated zest and juice of 2 oranges
150g ground almonds
150g quick-cook polenta
1 teaspoon baking powder

For the orange sugar syrup

juice of 2 oranges
3 tablespoons golden caster sugar

For the cranberry sauce

150g frozen cranberries, defrosted
75g golden caster sugar
juice of ½ orange

1. Preheat the oven to 160°C (140°C fan), 320°F, Gas 3. Butter and **line** the base of the tin with baking paper.

2. To make the cake, put the butter and caster sugar in a large mixing bowl or the bowl of a free-standing mixer and beat well until pale and creamy. Add the eggs, a little at a time, beating well between each addition to make sure that the egg is fully incorporated before adding the next bit.

3. Stir the vanilla extract and orange zest into the mixture, then **fold** in half the orange juice followed by half the ground almonds and half the polenta. Repeat this folding process with the remaining orange juice and ground almonds. Finally add the baking powder and remaining polenta, and fold again.

4. Spoon the cake mixture into your prepared tin and smooth the top with the back of a spoon. Bake for 1 hour, or until the top of the cake is golden brown and a skewer inserted into the centre of the cake comes out almost clean, with just a few crumbs attached.

5. While the cake is baking make the orange sugar syrup. Put the orange juice and sugar in a small pan and heat over a low heat until the sugar dissolves, stirring occasionally.

6. Remove the cake from the oven and prick holes all over the sponge with a skewer. Spoon over the orange sugar syrup and leave to cool completely.

7. For the cranberry sauce, put the cranberries, sugar and orange juice in a small pan over a low heat. Stir gently until the sugar has dissolved. Simmer for 5 minutes until the cranberries soften and the sauce turns syrupy.

8. Unclip the tin and serve the cake still on its base (or use a palette knife to slide it off the base onto a plate). Serve sliced, with the cranberry sauce.

Sticky Toffee Pudding

The addition of dates soaked in tea creates a moist pudding, which, when served with the rich toffee sauce, provides the best combination for a winter pudding.

HANDS-ON TIME:
20 minutes

BAKING TIME:
35–40 minutes

SERVES:
9

SPECIAL
EQUIPMENT:
20cm deep square
cake tin

METHOD USED:
Creamed sponge,
pages 22–23

200g dates
150ml hot tea, made with 1 tea bag
150g unsalted butter, softened
200g light muscovado sugar
3 eggs, at room temperature
200g self-raising flour
1 teaspoon bicarbonate of soda

For the toffee sauce
100g unsalted butter
200g light muscovado sugar
150ml double cream

1. Preheat the oven to 180°C (160°C fan), 350°F, Gas 4. Butter and **line** the tin with baking paper.

2. Chop the dates into small pieces then add to the hot tea. Put to one side to soak for 15 minutes while you make the sponge.

3. Cream together the softened butter and sugar in a large bowl with a wooden spoon (or use a hand-held electric mixer) until pale and light. Scrape down the sides of the bowl once or twice to ensure all of the mix is beaten. Add the eggs one at a time, beating well between each addition.

4. Sift the flour and bicarbonate of soda onto the creamed mix and then **fold** in with a rubber spatula until all of the flour is mixed in. Fold in the dates, along with any tea that hasn't soaked in, until you have a creamy cake batter. Pour into the prepared cake tin and bake for 35–40 minutes, or until the pudding is a deep golden brown. To check if it is cooked insert a skewer into the sponge; if it comes out with just a few moist crumbs the pudding is ready.

5. While the pudding is in the oven make the toffee sauce. Melt the butter in a small pan, then add the sugar and cream and cook over a low heat, stirring every now and then, until the sugar has dissolved. Once the sauce is smooth increase the heat and let it bubble for a couple of minutes.

6. Leave the pudding to cool for 5 minutes in the tin before turning out and cutting into squares. Serve warm with the hot toffee sauce.

Try Something Different

Replace the dates with the same amount of sultanas and add 100g roughly chopped walnuts.

Peach Melba

This traditional French dessert consists of peach halves poached in sugar syrup sitting on top of rounds of light whisked sponge with vanilla ice cream and a fresh raspberry coulis – summer on a plate.

Easy does it

HANDS-ON TIME:
30 minutes

BAKING TIME:
8–9 minutes

SERVES:
6

SPECIAL
EQUIPMENT:
20 × 30cm Swiss
roll tin,
8cm plain round
pastry cutter
(optional)

METHOD USED:
Whisked sponge,
pages 22–23

For the whisked sponge
butter, for greasing
3 medium eggs, at room temperature
100g caster sugar
100g plain flour

For the peaches
100g caster sugar
½ vanilla pod
3 peaches, halved and stoned

For the coulis
200g fresh raspberries
100g caster sugar
juice of ½ lemon

To serve
6 scoops of vanilla ice cream

1. Preheat the oven to 200°C (180°C fan), 400°F, Gas 6. Butter and **line** the Swiss roll tin with baking paper.

2. To make the whisked sponge, put the eggs and sugar in a large mixing bowl and whisk with a hand-held electric mixer (or use a free-standing mixer) for at least 5 minutes until the mixture becomes very pale and thick and leaves a ribbon-like trail when the whisk is lifted from the bowl.

3. Sift half the flour onto the mix and gently **fold** in, taking great care not to knock too much air out of the mix. Sift over the remaining flour and gently fold again, making sure you scrape right to the bottom of the bowl as the flour has a tendency to sink to the bottom when it's added.

4. Spoon the mix into the tin and spread it out right to the corners, smoothing the surface as you go. Bake for 8–9 minutes until golden and starting to shrink away from the edges of the tin.

Continued

5. While your sponge is in the oven, lay a piece of fresh baking paper on the work surface. Once the sponge is cooked turn it out of the tin onto the baking paper, then carefully peel off the lining paper.

6. Place a wire rack on top of the underside of the sponge, then flip the whole thing over so that the sponge is sitting right-side up on the rack. By cooling the sponge this way up you don't get the indents of the rack on the top of the cake.

7. For the peaches, put the 100g caster sugar in a pan large enough to hold the peach halves in a single layer. Split the ½ vanilla pod down its length with a small sharp knife then add to the pan with 300ml water. Heat over a low heat until the sugar has dissolved, stirring occasionally, then bring to a simmer. Add the 6 peach halves, skin side down. Simmer for 5 minutes then take off the heat, turn the peaches over so the skin is facing up and leave to cool in the poaching liquid for 5 minutes.

8. Take the peach halves out of the pan with a slotted spoon and remove the skins – they should peel away easily after cooking. Keep the poaching liquid for the finished pudding

9. For the coulis, put the 200g raspberries, 100g caster sugar and juice of ½ lemon in a small pan over a low heat. Heat through gently, until the sugar has dissolved, giving everything a stir once or twice. Bring to the boil and simmer for 1–2 minutes. Remove the pan from the heat and leave to cool for 5 minutes, then blitz with a hand-held blender. Pass the mixture through a sieve to remove the seeds and create a thick, smooth coulis.

10. To assemble, cut out six 8cm circles using a plain round pastry cutter, or by cutting round an upturned glass or bowl with a small sharp knife.

11. Put each circle of sponge onto a small plate, spoon over a little of the peachy sugar syrup, then top each one with a scoop of ice cream, a peach half and a finally a generous spoonful of raspberry coulis.

Christmas Pudding with Brandy Sauce

Christmas pudding tastes better if left to mature for a few months, so start your preparations early and make this rich, fruit-packed pudding in August or September.

For the Christmas pudding
100g sultanas
100g raisins
100g currants
100g stoned prunes, roughly chopped
175g soft dark brown sugar
finely grated zest of 1 orange
finely grated zest of 1 unwaxed lemon
50g plain flour
125g vegetable suet
100g fresh white breadcrumbs

½ teaspoon ground cinnamon
2 medium eggs, lightly beaten
75ml ginger wine
50ml brandy

For the brandy sauce
500ml full-fat milk
3 tablespoons cornflour
50g unsalted butter
50g caster sugar
3 tablespoons brandy

1. To make the pudding, lightly butter the pudding basin and **line** the base with a circle of baking paper. Place a trivet or upturned saucer in the bottom of a large pan (so that the basin isn't over the direct heat) and add enough water to come halfway up the sides of the pudding basin.

2. Put all the dry ingredients into a large mixing bowl and stir with a wooden spoon to combine, making sure that there are no clumps of zest, flour or sugar in the mixture.

3. Add the eggs, ginger wine and brandy, and stir again until you have a sticky mixture. Spoon the mixture into the pudding basin, pressing the mix down well as you go to make sure that there are no gaps, then smooth the top with the back of a spoon.

Continued

Try Something Different

Christmas puddings are traditionally made on Stir-up Sunday, which is the Sunday before the start of Advent. Everyone in the family gives the pudding a stir and a sixpence or two are added to the mixture – whoever gets a sixpence in their pudding on Christmas Day will have good luck! If you want to do something similar, sterilise a few coins and add them to the mixture in step 3. Take care when eating the pudding as you don't want a trip to the dentist at Christmas and do not be tempted to reheat the pudding in a microwave!

4. Take a double layer of baking paper that is about 10cm wider than the diameter of the pudding basin (you need a double layer to protect the pudding as it is steamed for so long). Fold a pleat in the centre of the paper (to allow room for the pudding to rise) and then place this on top of the basin.

5. Take a piece of foil the same size and again fold a pleat down the centre and place on top of the baking paper. Push the foil down around the top edge of the basin, then take a piece of string and tie around the foil and baking paper under the rim of the basin; tie it securely as it will need to take the weight of the pudding when you are lifting the basin in and out of the pan. Trim the foil and baking paper so that it doesn't dip in the water as the pudding cooks.

6. Take another piece of string and use it to create a handle across the top of the basin, by passing it under the tied string on each side and then securing it in the middle with a knot, leaving enough give for you to get your hand under. Bring the pan of water to the boil.

7. Place the pudding in the pan on top of the trivet or saucer, making sure that the water comes halfway up the sides of the basin. Cover the pan with a tight-fitting lid and simmer gently for 3 hours. Check the level of water every now and then and top up when needed with boiling water from a kettle.

8. At the end of the cooking time take the pudding out of the water and leave it in the basin to cool completely. Remove the baking paper and foil and put on a fresh piece of each, as explained in step 4 but without the pleats. Store in a cool, dark place until Christmas day.

9. On Christmas day, steam the pudding as above for 2 hours. Remove from the pan and set to one side for 10 minutes while you make the brandy sauce.

10. Put the 500ml milk in a small pan over a low heat, mix the 3 tablespoons cornflour with a little of the milk to form a smooth paste and add this to the pan. Add the 50g butter and 50g sugar to the pan and bring to a simmer, stirring constantly until the sauce thickens.

Simmer gently for 5 minutes, stirring occasionally, then add the brandy, stir again and pour into a warmed jug to serve.

11. When you're ready to serve, heat the 50ml brandy in a small pan until steaming. Turn the pudding out onto a serving plate and remove the circle of baking paper. Take the pudding to the table, pour the warmed brandy over the top of the pudding and set light to it with a long match at the base of the pudding so that the blue flames flicker up the sides. Serve once the flames have gone out.

Chocolate Mousse Cake

A just-baked chocolate cake with a mousse-like middle that will allow you to perfect your folding-in skills. It is very rich so serve in small slices – a little goes a long way.

300g dark chocolate, preferably 70 per cent cocoa solids
150g unsalted butter
4 medium eggs, at room temperature, separated
150g golden caster sugar
1 tablespoon icing sugar, for dusting
150g redcurrants, to serve

Easy does it

HANDS-ON TIME:
25 minutes

BAKING TIME:
45 minutes

SERVES:
8–10

SPECIALIST
EQUIPMENT:
22cm springclip tin

1. Preheat the oven to 180°C (160°C fan), 350°F, Gas 4. Butter the cake tin and **line** the base and sides with baking paper.

2. Break the chocolate into small pieces and place with the butter in a heatproof bowl to **melt** it. Set the bowl over a pan of gently simmering water, making sure that the bottom of the bowl doesn't touch the water, or melt in the microwave in short bursts, stirring occasionally until the chocolate is completely smooth. Put to one side to cool.

3. In a large mixing bowl, whisk together the egg yolks and caster sugar until thick and pale and doubled in size.

4. In a separate bowl, **whisk** the egg whites to **stiff peaks**, using either a free-standing mixer or clean whisks on your hand-held electric mixer. You can check if they are stiff enough by turning the bowl upside down – the egg whites shouldn't fall out.

5. **Fold** the cooled chocolate and butter into the egg yolks, then add a spoonful of egg whites and fold that in to loosen the mixture slightly before folding in the rest of the egg whites. Fold as gently as possible so that you don't knock too much air out, as you want the mixture to be as light as possible.

6. Pour the mix into your prepared tin. Bake for about 45 minutes until the cake has just set but is still gooey in the middle (use a cocktail stick inserted in the centre to check). Leave to cool completely in the tin, then unclip the tin and carefully peel off the baking paper. Place on a serving plate, still on its base, and dust with icing sugar before serving. Serve cut into slices topped with the redcurrants.

Fig and Frangipane Tart

A sweet pastry case makes a lovely base for this almond and fig-topped tart and is a great introduction to blind baking.

HANDS-ON TIME:
30 minutes, plus chilling

BAKING TIME:
55 minutes–1 hour

SERVES:
10

SPECIALIST EQUIPMENT:
23cm round loose-bottomed fluted flan tin, 3cm deep

METHODS USED:
Rich shortcrust pastry, page 25;
Creamed sponge, pages 22–23

For the rich shortcrust pastry
250g plain flour, plus extra for dusting
50g icing sugar, plus extra for dusting
125g chilled unsalted butter, diced
2 medium egg yolks
1 tablespoon of ice-cold water

For the filling
150g unsalted butter, softened
150g caster sugar
3 medium eggs, at room temperature, lightly beaten
150g ground almonds
1 teaspoon almond extract
4 fresh figs, quartered

1. First, make the rich shortcrust pastry. Sift the flour and icing sugar into a large bowl, add the butter and mix gently to coat the butter pieces in flour. **Rub in** until the mixture resembles fine breadcrumbs. Add the egg yolks and water and stir in using a round-bladed knife, adding a little more water if needed to create a soft dough. Gently bring the dough together with your hands and shape into a ball. (Or make the pastry in a food-processor.)

2. Flatten the ball of dough into a thick disc, wrap in clingfilm and chill in the fridge for 20 minutes.

3. **Roll out** the dough on a lightly floured surface into a circle large enough to line the flan tin and about the thickness of a £1 coin. Give the pastry a quarter turn every now and then to stop it sticking to the surface.

4. **Line** the tin with the pastry, easing the pastry into the edges. Run the rolling pin over the top of the flan tin to cut off the excess pastry, then press the pastry into the flutes of the tin using the side of your finger. Prick the base with a fork and chill again in

the fridge for 20 minutes. This second chilling will stop the pastry from shrinking back as it bakes.

5. Preheat the oven to 200°C (180°C fan), 400°F, Gas 6. Line the pastry case with baking paper, then fill with baking beans or uncooked rice and **blind bake** for 10 minutes. Remove the paper and beans and bake for another 5 minutes to allow the base of the case to cook (it should feel dry and sandy to touch). Remove from the oven and put to one side to cool while you make the filling. Lower the oven temperature to 180°C (160°C fan), 350°F, Gas 4.

6. For the filling, cream together the butter and sugar in a large bowl with a wooden spoon (or use a hand-held electric mixer) until pale and fluffy, then add the eggs a little at a time, beating well between each addition. **Fold** in the ground almonds and almond extract, then spoon this mixture into the pastry case. Scatter the fig quarters over the top, then bake for 40–45 minutes, or until the top is golden brown and firm to the touch. Serve warm or cold, dusted with icing sugar.

Queen of Puddings

This traditional English pudding is a great combination of a creamy base topped with jam and **meringue** and is a chance to try out your piping skills.

For the base
75g slightly stale brioche
600ml full-fat milk
50g caster sugar
4 medium egg yolks

For the jam
300g fresh blackberries
300g caster sugar
juice of ½ lemon

For the meringue
4 medium egg whites, at room temperature
240g caster sugar

Easy does it

HANDS-ON TIME:
30 minutes

BAKING TIME:
45–50 minutes

SERVES:
8

SPECIAL
EQUIPMENT:
15 × 25cm shallow
baking dish, roasting
tin, piping bag,
2cm plain round
nozzle

METHOD USED:
French meringue,
page 28

1. To make the base, break the brioche into chunks and whizz in a food-processor to fine crumbs. Butter the baking dish and tip the crumbs into it.

2. In a small pan warm the milk and sugar and stir until the sugar has dissolved. Put the egg yolks in a mixing bowl and whisk lightly, then add the milk to the yolks, whisking all the time. Pour this custard over the brioche crumbs and leave them to soak for 30 minutes.

3. While the crumbs are soaking, make the jam. Put the blackberries, caster sugar and lemon juice in a large pan and heat gently until the sugar has dissolved. Then bring the jam to the boil and let it bubble rapidly for about 10 minutes until it reaches 105°C (220°F) on a kitchen thermometer. Leave in the pan to cool. Preheat the oven to 170°C (150°C fan), 325°F, Gas 3 and boil the kettle.

4. Put the baking dish in a roasting tin and fill with boiling water to come halfway up the sides of the dish. Bake for 30 minutes until golden and the custard looks set, but with a slight wobble in the centre. Remove from the roasting tin and leave to cool.

5. To make the meringue, put the egg whites into a large bowl or the bowl of a free-standing mixer and **whisk** until you have **stiff peaks**. Add the caster sugar a spoonful at time, whisking well between each addition. Once you have added all the sugar and you have a thick and glossy meringue, use it to **fill a large piping bag** fitted with a 2cm plain round nozzle.

6. Spread the jam over the custard and brioche base, then **pipe** the meringue on top in neat rows. Return the pudding to the oven and bake for 15–20 minutes, or until the meringue is golden and crisp. Serve warm or cold.

Try Something Different

For a more traditional Queen of Puddings, use white bread for the breadcrumbs and replace the blackberries with the same amount of raspberries.

Almond Tuile Biscuits and Blackberry Sorbet

These delicate, shaped almond biscuits are a great way to turn a simple sorbet into an impressive dessert and this deep purple blackberry sorbet is a great way of using up a glut of fruit in the autumn.

HANDS-ON TIME:
30 minutes

HANDS-OFF TIME:
4 hours, plus
overnight freezing

BAKING TIME:
10 minutes

SERVES:
4

SPECIAL
EQUIPMENT:
2 large baking sheets

For the blackberry sorbet
150g granulated sugar
½ vanilla pod
500g fresh blackberries, plus extra
for serving
juice of 1 lemon
fresh mint leaves, to garnish

For the almond tuile biscuits
1 medium egg white
60g icing sugar
30g plain flour
30g unsalted butter, melted and
cooled
50g flaked almonds

1. For the sorbet, put the sugar in a medium pan with 150ml water over a low heat, stirring every now and then until the sugar has dissolved. Slit the vanilla pod lengthways, add it to the pan with the blackberries and lemon juice and bring to the boil. Simmer for 2–3 minutes until the fruit has softened.

2. Remove from the heat and leave to cool for 10 minutes, then remove the vanilla pod and purée the blackberry mix with a hand-held blender. Pass through a sieve to remove the pips and leave to cool completely.

3. Pour into a shallow freezer container, cover with a lid and freeze for 2 hours until it starts to go slushy around the edges. Beat the mix with a fork to break up the ice crystals, making sure you scrape right round the edges of the container – this will ensure you get a nice smooth sorbet. Return to the freezer for another hour, beat again then repeat once more before leaving to freeze completely, ideally overnight.

4. For the tuile biscuits, put the egg white in a mixing bowl and lightly **whisk** until frothy. Sift in the icing sugar and whisk again, then sift in the flour, whisk again and finally whisk in the cooled butter until you have a smooth mix.

5. Put in the fridge to rest for 30 minutes. Preheat the oven to 170°C (150°C fan), 325°F, Gas 3 and line two large baking sheets with baking paper.

6. **Fold** the almonds into the biscuit mix then spoon a dessertspoon of the mixture onto a baking sheet and spread into a thin disc. Repeat to make four discs, leaving plenty of space between each one. Bake one tray at a time for about 10 minutes until they start to turn golden brown at the edges. Slide a palette knife under each tuile and drape over a lightly oiled rolling pin. Press the edges down to create the curl. Work quickly as the tuiles harden as they cool. Repeat this baking and shaping with the rest of the mixture.

7. To serve, take the sorbet out of the freezer and leave in the fridge for 15 minutes to soften slightly, scoop and serve alongside the tuiles. Decorate with fresh blackberries and mint sprigs.

Apple and Stem Ginger Lattice Tart

This fruit-packed tart spiced with stem ginger lets you practise your lattice skills and hone your **shortcrust pastry** all in one.

Easy does it

HANDS-ON TIME:
35 minutes

BAKING TIME:
40–45 minutes

SERVES:
6–8

SPECIAL
EQUIPMENT:
20cm shallow pie
dish

METHOD USED:
Shortcrust pastry,
pages 24–25

For the pastry
250g plain flour, plus extra for dusting
½ teaspoon salt
125g chilled unsalted butter, diced
2 tablespoons milk, for brushing

For the filling
1kg cooking apples
100g golden caster sugar
2 balls stem ginger, finely diced

1. First make the pastry. Put the flour and salt into a large mixing bowl and **rub in** the butter until the mixture resembles fine breadcrumbs. Pour in about 4 tablespoons of cold water and stir in with a round-bladed knife to form a soft dough. (Or make the pastry in a food-processor.) Shape into a flat disc, wrap in clingfilm and chill in the fridge for 20 minutes.

2. For the filling, peel and core 750g of the apples then cut into thick slices and place in a large pan with the sugar. Cook over a medium heat for about 10 minutes until soft and fluffy, stirring occasionally to stop the apples catching on the bottom of the pan. Remove from the heat and leave to cool.

3. **Roll out** two-thirds of the dough on a lightly floured surface into a circle the thickness of a £1 coin and large enough to **line** the pie dish with a slight overhang. Line the dish with the pastry, gently easing it into the edges and press the top edge down around the rim. Trim the excess pastry using a small, sharp knife. Gather up the pastry trimmings, add to the remaining pastry and re-wrap in clingfilm. Chill both the lined dish and the pastry trimmings for 20 minutes. Preheat the oven to 200°C (180°C fan), 400°F, Gas 6.

4. Peel and core the remaining 250g apples and cut into chunks. Stir into the cold cooked apple along with the diced stem ginger. Spoon into the pastry case.

5. Roll out the remaining pastry into a rectangle, then using a pizza cutter or pastry wheel, cut into ten long strips about 1cm wide. Brush the edge of the pastry case with a little milk. Lay five of the strips evenly spaced over the top of the apple filling, then lay the other five strips going across the first in a lattice pattern, taking each strip over and under the strips to interlock them as you go. Press the ends down and trim them. Re-roll the scraps of pastry, then cut out an apple shape and a couple of leaves and place in the centre of the lattice work, brush all the pastry with milk. Bake for 40–45 minutes, or until the top is golden. Serve warm with custard.

Try Something Different

To make a pie with a plain pastry lid, make the pastry as above but using 300g flour and 150g butter. Roll the remaining pastry into a circle big enough to cover the dish. Lay the pastry circle over the apples, press the edges to seal, trim away the excess and cut a hole for the steam to escape.

Tropical Pavlova

Crisp baked **meringue** with a gooey centre topped with Chantilly cream, fresh mango and passion fruit – an ideal way to perfect your meringue-making skills.

HANDS-ON TIME:
30 minutes

HANDS-OFF TIME:
1 hour

BAKING TIME:
1 hour

SERVES:
8

SPECIAL
EQUIPMENT:
large baking sheet

METHOD USED:
French meringue,
page 28

For the meringue
4 medium egg whites, at room temperature
250g caster sugar
1 teaspoon cornflour
1 teaspoon white wine vinegar

For the filling
300ml double cream, well chilled
2 tablespoons icing sugar
1 mango
2 passion fruit

1. Preheat the oven to 120°C (100°C fan), 250°F, Gas ½. **Line** the baking sheet with baking paper.

2. For the meringue, put the egg whites into a large, spotlessly clean mixing bowl or the bowl of a free-standing mixer and **whisk** until they form **stiff peaks**. Add the caster sugar, a tablespoon at a time, whisking well between each addition to make sure that each batch of sugar has dissolved before adding the next. Once you've added about half the sugar, whisk in the cornflour and vinegar, then whisk in the rest of the sugar, a tablespoon at a time, as before.

3. Draw a 22cm circle onto the piece of baking paper, turn it over and stick it down to the baking sheet using a dab of meringue at each corner. Tip the meringue onto the baking sheet and spread out to roughly fill the circle, creating sides and a dip in the middle to allow space to fill with cream and fruit. Swirl the top of the sides with a skewer a little to create a pattern.

4. Bake in the oven for 1 hour until crisp and firm but not coloured. Turn off the oven and wedge open the door with a tea towel, then leave the pavlova to cool in the oven for another hour. This will stop it cracking too much as it cools.

5. Remove the meringue from the oven, peel off the baking paper and place carefully on a serving plate.

6. For the filling, put the cream into a large mixing bowl, sift over the icing sugar and **whip** until **soft peaks** have formed. Spoon into the centre of the meringue case.

7. Peel the mango, cut the flesh away from the stone, then cut into 2cm cubes. Scatter these over the cream, then top with the flesh and juice from the passion fruit. Serve immediately.

Try Something Different

You can make this pavlova with any soft fresh fruit – try 100g each of raspberries, blueberries and strawberries.

Steamed Stem Ginger Puddings with Custard

Steaming these individual puddings flavoured with stem ginger gives a light and fluffy texture that is great served with the ginger wine-laced custard.

HANDS-ON TIME:
40 minutes

STEAMING TIME:
30 minutes

MAKES:
6

SPECIAL
EQUIPMENT:
6 × 150ml capacity
pudding basins,
2 steamers (optional)

METHOD USED:
Creamed sponge,
pages 22–23

For the steamed stem ginger puddings

4 balls stem ginger in syrup, finely diced
4 tablespoons ginger syrup from the jar
150g unsalted butter, softened
150g soft light brown sugar
3 medium eggs, at room temperature, lightly beaten

150g self-raising flour
1 teaspoon ground ginger

For the custard

4 medium egg yolks
2 tablespoons soft light brown sugar
1 tablespoon cornflour
400ml full-fat milk
100ml ginger wine

1. Lightly butter the pudding basins and **line** the base of each with a small circle of baking paper. Fill the bottom of a steamer with water, or fill a large shallow pan so that the water comes halfway up the sides of the basins.

2. Divide half the diced stem ginger between the six pudding basins and pour 1 teaspoon of the syrup on top.

3. Cream together the butter and sugar in a large mixing bowl with a wooden spoon until pale and fluffy (or use a free-standing mixer). Add the eggs a little at a time, beating well between each addition. Sift the flour and ground ginger into the bowl with the remaining stem ginger and syrup and **fold** in.

4. Spoon the mixture into the pudding basins and smooth with the back of a spoon. Cut six squares of baking paper and foil large enough to cover the tops of the basins with about 2cm extra around each side. Put a square of baking paper followed by a square of foil on top of a basin and push the foil down around the edge to seal. Repeat with the other puddings. Bring the water in the steamer or pan to the boil.

5. Put the basins in the steamer or pan of water in a single layer (you may need two). Steam for 30 minutes, by which time the puddings should have risen. To test if they are cooked, peel back the foil and paper and insert a skewer into the centre; it should come out clean. If they are not quite done, fold back the paper and foil, and steam for 5 minutes.

6. While the puddings are steaming make the custard. Lightly whisk the egg yolks, sugar and cornflour in a bowl to a smooth paste. Heat the milk and ginger wine in a pan over a low heat until just steaming, then pour over the egg mixture, whisking all the time. Return the custard to the pan over a low heat for about 10 minutes, stirring, until thick enough to coat the back of a spoon; .

7. Run a small palette knife around the edge of each basin to loosen the puddings, then turn out onto a plate. Remove the baking paper and serve with the hot custard.

Cherry and Chocolate Knickerbocker Glory

This pudding introduces you to the skill of making ice cream, layered with a rich chocolate brownie and poached cherries, topped with a dollop of whipped cream.

Needs a little skill

HANDS-ON TIME:
50 minutes

HANDS-OFF TIME:
4 hours, plus
overnight freezing

BAKING TIME:
25–30 minutes

MAKES:
4

SPECIAL
EQUIPMENT:
ice-cream machine
(optional),
20 × 30cm baking
tin, about 3–4cm
deep

For the vanilla ice cream
600ml full-fat milk
1 vanilla pod, slit lengthways
6 medium egg yolks
175g caster sugar
600ml double cream

For the brownie
300g dark chocolate, chopped
200g unsalted butter, plus extra for greasing
4 medium eggs, at room temperature
300g golden caster sugar
150g plain flour
150g dried cherries

For the cherries
300g frozen cherries, defrosted
50g golden caster sugar
1 tablespoon lemon juice

To serve
200ml double cream, well chilled

1. For the ice cream, heat the milk and vanilla pod in a pan over a low heat until it starts to simmer. In a large mixing bowl whisk the egg yolks and sugar together until pale and slowly add the warmed milk to the bowl, whisking all the time.

2. Pour the mixture back into the pan and heat gently for about 10 minutes until the custard thickens enough to coat the back of a spoon. Remove from the heat and leave to cool. Once completely cold remove and discard the vanilla pod.
Continued

3. Freeze the ice cream. To freeze ice cream without a machine, transfer the mixture to a wide plastic container with an airtight lid. You need the mixture to be no deeper than about 5cm, so you can beat it easily. Place in the freezer for 2 hours. Take the ice cream out of the freezer and scrape it into a bowl. Beat for a few minutes with a hand-held blender to break up the ice crystals. **Whip** the cream until **soft peaks** form and **fold** this into the frozen custard, then return the mixture to the container. Freeze for another hour, then mix well with a fork and leave to freeze completely.

4. If you have an ice-cream machine, it will churn the mixture as it freezes. Whip the cream to soft peaks and fold this into the chilled custard before transferring to the ice-cream machine – follow the manufacturer's instructions and then transfer to a plastic container with an airtight lid and store in the freezer until needed.

5. For the brownie, preheat the oven to 180°C (160°C fan), 350°F, Gas 4. Butter the tin and **line** with baking paper.

6. Place the 300g dark chocolate and 200g butter in a heatproof bowl to **melt**, either set over a pan of gently simmering water (making sure the bottom of the bowl doesn't touch the water) or in the microwave. Stir gently until smooth, then put to one side to cool.

7. In a large mixing bowl, whisk together the 4 eggs and 300g sugar until pale and thick. Whisk the cooled chocolate and butter into the eggs, then gently fold in the 150g flour and 150g dried cherries. Pour into the prepared tin and smooth the surface with the back of a spoon.

8. Bake in the oven for 25–30 minutes until the brownie is firm to the touch and comes away slightly from the sides of the tin. Leave to cool in the tin for 10 minutes, then lift out and place on a wire rack to cool completely.

9. For the cherries, put the 300g cherries, 50g golden caster sugar and 1 tablespoon of lemon juice in a small pan. Heat gently until the sugar has dissolved, then bring to a simmer and cook for 5 minutes. Remove from the heat and leave to cool.

10. Put the 200ml double cream into a large bowl and whip until soft peaks form; chill until needed.

11. You're now ready to assemble the puddings. Put the ice cream in the fridge for 20 minutes before serving to make the ice cream easier to scoop. Cut the brownies into small squares that will fit in your serving glasses – some might be bigger than others if the glasses get wider at the top. Put a spoonful of cherries in the bottom of each glass, top with a square of brownie and a scoop of ice cream. Repeat the layers once more, saving four of the cherries. Finish off with a dollop of whipped cream, a cherry and a last drizzle of cherry syrup. Serve immediately.

Chocolate and Orange Tarts with Cointreau Cream

Move your pastry skills on to lining individual tart tins with a chocolate pastry, filled with orange custard and topped with candied peel.

For the pastry
120g unsalted butter, softened
70g icing sugar
I medium egg
200g plain flour
40g cocoa powder

For the custard
4 medium egg yolks
50g caster sugar
150ml full-fat milk

150ml double cream
finely grated zest of I orange

For the candied peel
I orange (peel only)
100g caster sugar

For the Cointreau cream
200ml double cream, well chilled
2 tablespoons icing sugar
I tablespoon Cointreau

HANDS-ON TIME:
45 minutes, plus
chilling

BAKING TIME:
30 minutes

MAKES:
6

SPECIAL
EQUIPMENT:
6 round 10cm
individual loose-
bottomed tart tins,
2cm deep,
baking sheet

METHOD USED:
Pâte sucrée,
page 26

1. First make the pastry. Put the butter and icing sugar in a mixing bowl and beat with a wooden spoon until soft and creamy. Beat in the egg, then sift in the flour and cocoa powder and mix until you have a soft dough. Shape into a flat disc, then wrap in clingfilm and chill in the fridge for 20 minutes.

2. Divide the pastry into six equal portions, then **roll out** each piece, on a lightly floured surface into a 13cm circle about the thickness of a £1 coin. **Line** the flan tins, pressing the pastry into the edges with a small ball of the dough.
Continued

3. Roll your rolling pin over the top of the tart tins to cut off any excess pastry and prick the bases with a fork. Put on a baking sheet and chill in the fridge for 15 minutes.

4. Preheat the oven to 200°C (180°C fan), 400°F, Gas 6. Line each pastry case with baking paper and fill with a handful of baking beans or uncooked rice. **Blind bake** for 10 minutes, then remove the paper and beans and bake for a further 5 minutes, until the pastry feels dry and sandy to touch. Remove from the oven and reduce the temperature to 180°C (160°C fan), 350°F, Gas 4.

5. While the pastry cases are baking, make your custard. Whisk the 4 egg yolks and 50g caster sugar together in a mixing bowl until smooth. Gently heat

the 150ml milk and 150ml cream in a pan over a low heat until it just starts to steam. Remove from the heat and whisk into the egg yolks until fully blended and you have a smooth custard. Pour through a sieve into a jug and stir in the finely grated zest of 1 orange.

6. Put the baking sheet of pastry cases on the middle shelf of the oven and fill each one to just below the top with custard. Bake in the oven for 15 minutes until the custard is just set with a slight wobble in the middle. Leave to cool in their tins.

7. For the candied peel, peel the skin off the orange with a potato peeler so you just get the peel and none of the bitter white pith; slice into thin strips. Bring a small amount of water to the boil in a

pan, then blanch the strips of orange peel for a couple of minutes and drain. Put the 100g caster sugar and 100ml water in the pan, and heat gently over a low heat to dissolve the sugar, then add the orange strips and simmer for 10 minutes until they are translucent. Remove the strips from the sugar syrup using a slotted spoon and lay out on a piece of baking paper to dry.

8. For the Cointreau cream, put the 200ml double cream, 2 tablespoons of icing sugar and 1 tablespoon of Cointreau in a large mixing bowl and **whip** until you have **soft peaks**.

9. To serve, remove the tarts from their tins and place each one on a small plate. Top with a few pieces of candied orange peel and a large dollop of Cointreau cream.

Baked Vanilla Cheesecake with Blueberry Jelly

This New York-style cheesecake is gently baked to create a dense, creamy filling that is then topped with a thin layer of blueberry jelly to provide the perfect contrast of flavours and textures.

Needs a little skill

HANDS-ON TIME:
30 minutes, plus chilling

BAKING TIME:
45 minutes

SERVES:
12

SPECIAL EQUIPMENT:
23cm springclip cake tin

For the vanilla cheesecake
150g digestive biscuits
75g unsalted butter
900g cream cheese, at room temperature
200g caster sugar
200ml soured cream
3 tablespoons plain flour
3 medium eggs, plus 1 egg yolk
2 teaspoons vanilla extract

For the blueberry jelly
200g fresh blueberries
100g caster sugar
2 sheets of leaf gelatine (see page 14)

1. Preheat the oven to 180°C (160°C fan), 350°F, Gas 4. Butter and **line** the base of the tin with baking paper.

2. Put the digestive biscuits in a plastic food bag, seal the top and crush with a rolling pin to create fine crumbs (you can whizz them in a food-processor, but bashing them is quick and easy and creates a lot less washing up). Melt the butter in a pan over a low heat, add the biscuit crumbs and stir to coat. Tip the biscuits into the prepared tin and smooth down to cover the base; if you press them down using a potato masher you'll get a nice even layer. Bake in the oven for 10 minutes, then put to one side to cool while you make the topping. Reduce the oven temperature to 160°C (140°C fan), 320°F, Gas 2.

3. Put the cream cheese (taking it out of the fridge a couple of hours beforehand will make it easier to mix) and sugar in a large mixing bowl. Beat together with a wooden spoon until smooth. Add the soured cream and flour, and beat again.
Continued

4. Add the 3 eggs to the cream cheese mixture one at time, beating gently after each addition – you don't want to add too much air into the mixture as this will create bubbles that will affect the texture of the cheesecake. Finally, add the egg yolk and 2 teaspoons vanilla extract and beat until you have a smooth, creamy mixture. Pour onto the cooled biscuit base, then tap the tin on your work surface a couple of times to smooth the top and pop any air bubbles.

5. Bake in the oven for 45 minutes until just set, with a slight wobble in the centre. The top should still be pale and only slightly golden around the edge. Leave to cool in the oven, propping the door open with a tea towel; this will stop the cheesecake from cracking as it cools.

6. For the blueberry jelly, put the 200g blueberries and 100g caster sugar in a pan over a low heat and heat gently until the sugar has melted, stirring occasionally. Increase the heat and simmer for 5 minutes until the blueberries are nice and soft.

7. Remove from the heat and use a hand-held blender to blitz the berries, then pass this purée through a sieve. Soak the 2 sheets of gelatine in a bowl of cold water for 10 minutes to soften.

8. Rinse out the pan and return the sieved blueberry purée to the pan and heat through gently, then remove from the heat. Lift the softened gelatine leaves from the cold water and squeeze gently to remove the excess water, then add to the pan and stir until the gelatine has melted. Pour the jelly into a jug and put to one side to cool completely.

9. Carefully pour the jelly on top of the cooled cheesecake to cover the surface in a nice even layer. Chill in the fridge for 2–3 hours until jelly has set.

10. To serve, unclip the tin and carefully slide a spatula under the cheesecake to remove it from the base and peel off the baking paper.

Pineapple Tarte Tatin

This tropical twist on a French classic has golden pastry baked on top of caramelised pineapple and is a great way for you to try out your **puff pastry**-making skills.

For the puff pastry
250g strong white flour, plus extra
for dusting
½ teaspoon salt
225g chilled unsalted butter
1 teaspoon lemon juice

For the pineapple topping
1 small pineapple
100g caster sugar
25g unsalted butter

HANDS-ON TIME:
50 minutes, plus
chilling

BAKING TIME:
30–35 minutes

SERVES:
4–6

**SPECIAL
EQUIPMENT:**
20cm round tarte
Tatin tin

METHOD USED:
Puff pastry,
pages 26–27

1. For the pastry, put the flour and salt into a mixing bowl. Dice 25g of the butter and use your fingertips to **rub in** to the flour. Add the lemon juice and 150ml cold water and stir together with a round-bladed knife to form a soft dough. Tip onto a lightly floured surface and knead for 2–3 minutes until smooth. Put the dough into a clean bowl, cover with clingfilm and chill in the fridge for 30 minutes.

2. Place the remaining butter between two sheets of baking paper and use a rolling pin to shape the butter into a square about 10cm across. Tip the dough onto a lightly floured surface and **roll out** into a square about 20cm across. Place the square of butter onto the centre of the dough, positioned so that the corners of the butter are pointing at the middle of the sides of the dough. Take care not to handle the butter too much as this will soften it. Fold each of the corners of the dough over the butter so that they meet in the middle and encase the butter.
Continued

Try Something Different

For a more traditional tarte Tatin, replace the pineapple with six eating apples such as Braeburn. Peel, core and quarter them and cook as above.

3. Give the dough a quarter turn so that a straight edge of the square is facing you. Make three indents in the dough with your rolling pin across the top, middle and bottom of the square, and roll into a rectangle about 45 × 15cm. Then fold the bottom third up and the top third down, brushing off any excess flour from the pastry as you fold.

4. Give the dough another quarter turn and repeat the rolling and folding process. Wrap the pastry in clingfilm and chill in the fridge for 30 minutes.

5. Repeat the above rolling, folding and chilling process twice more, so that in all you have rolled and folded the dough six times. Chill for a final 30 minutes before using.

6. For the topping, peel the pineapple and remove any eyes with the tip of a potato peeler. Cut into six slices and remove the centre of each circle using an apple corer. Pat dry on kitchen paper.

7. Put the 100g sugar in a large frying pan with 2 tablespoons of water. Place over a low heat until the sugar has dissolved. Swirl the pan gently every now and then to help the sugar to dissolve evenly. Once you have a clear liquid in the pan increase the heat and boil until the sugar syrup turns a deep caramel colour; again, swirl the pan once or twice once the caramel starts to form to stop it from burning round the edges (don't be tempted to stir the contents of the pan as you won't get a clear caramel). Add the 25g butter to the caramel.

8. Add the pineapple slices to the pan, stir to coat in the caramel and cook for 5 minutes to soften slightly. Remove the slices from the pan and arrange them in the base of the tin in a circle, with the slices overlapping slightly. Pour the caramel over the slices. Preheat the oven to 200°C (180°C fan), 400°F, Gas 6.

9. Cut the pastry in half, and wrap the other half in clingfilm and chill or freeze to use another time. (It is difficult to make puff pastry in smaller quantities.) On a lightly floured surface roll out the pastry to a circle that is slightly larger than the diameter of the tin – about 22cm – and about the thickness of a £1 coin. Prick the pastry all over with a fork and then lay over the pineapple chunks.

10. Tuck the edges of the pastry into the dish so that the fruit is completely encased.

11. Bake for 30–35 minutes until the pastry is well risen, crisp and golden. Remove from the oven and leave to cool for 5–10 minutes so that the caramel can settle and stop bubbling.

12. Loosen the edges of the pastry away from the tin with a small round-bladed knife, then place an inverted plate on top of the tart tin and quickly turn the tin over onto the plate (wear oven gloves for this as the tin will still be very hot). Let the tart fall out onto the plate and leave it for a minute so that all the caramel comes out of the tin. Serve warm with whipped cream or ice cream.

Raspberry
Trifle

The base of this oh-so-English dessert is a Swiss roll filled with raspberry jam, allowing you to perfect your **whisked sponge**, as well as practise rolling. It is topped with a rich vanilla custard and a generous pile of softly whipped cream.

Needs a little skill

HANDS-ON TIME:
50–60 minutes

HANDS-OFF TIME:
1–2 hours chilling

BAKING TIME:
8–9 minutes

SERVES:
8

SPECIAL EQUIPMENT:
20 × 30cm Swiss roll tin,
20cm trifle bowl

METHOD USED:
Whisked sponge,
pages 23–24

For the Swiss roll
3 medium eggs, at room temperature
100g caster sugar, plus extra for sprinkling
100g plain flour

For the raspberry jam
200g raspberries
200g granulated sugar
juice of ½ lemon
1 tablespoon pectin

For the custard
6 medium egg yolks
1 tablespoon cornflour
50g caster sugar
300ml full-fat milk
300ml double cream
1 vanilla pod, slit lengthways

To finish
60ml sherry
600ml double cream, well chilled
2 tablespoons icing sugar
50g fresh raspberries

1. Preheat the oven to 200°C (180°C fan), 400°F, Gas 6. Butter and **line** the tin with baking paper.

2. For the Swiss roll, put the eggs and sugar in a large mixing bowl or the bowl of a free-standing mixer and whisk for at least 5 minutes until the mixture becomes very pale and thick and leaves a ribbon-like trail when the whisk is lifted.
Continued

3. Sift 50g of the flour onto the mixture and gently **fold** in, taking great care not to knock too much air out of the mix. Sift over the remaining 50g flour and gently fold again, making sure you scrape right to the bottom of the bowl as the flour has a tendency to sink to the bottom when it's added.

4. Spoon the mixture into the prepared tin and spread it out right to the corners, smoothing the surface as you go. Bake in the oven for 8–9 minutes until golden and starting to shrink away from the edges of the tin.

5. While the Swiss roll is cooking, place a piece of baking paper on a wire rack and sprinkle with a little caster sugar. When the sponge is cooked turn it out of the tin onto the baking paper on the rack with a short edge facing you. Peel off the lining paper, then with a small knife make a shallow cut parallel with the short edge nearest you, all the way across the width of the sponge and about 2cm up from the edge. This will ensure you get a neat roll. Start to roll up the sponge with the paper. Leave on the wire rack to cool.

6. For the jam, put the 200g raspberries, 200g sugar, juice of ½ lemon and 1 tablespoon of pectin in a pan. Heat gently over a low heat until the sugar has dissolved, then increase the heat, bring to the boil and boil for about 10 minutes, or until it reaches 105°C (220°F) on a kitchen thermometer. Put to one side to cool.

7. For the custard, in a large bowl whisk together the 6 egg yolks, 1 tablespoon of cornflour and 50g sugar. Put the 300ml full-fat milk, 300ml double cream and slit vanilla pod in a pan, and heat over a low heat until it begins to simmer. Pour the hot milk over the egg mixture, whisking as you pour, then return the custard to the pan. Heat over a low heat, stirring continuously until the custard thickens; this could take about 10 minutes, but don't rush it or the eggs could curdle. Pour into a bowl, cover the surface with clingfilm to prevent a skin forming and leave to cool.

8. Carefully unroll the Swiss roll and remove the baking paper. Spread the cooled jam over the sponge in an even layer. Re-roll and cut into slices about 1.5cm thick. Arrange the slices in the base of the trifle dish and spoon over the 60ml sherry. Pour the cooled custard over the base and chill for 1–2 hours.

9. Put the 600ml double cream and 2 tablespoons of icing sugar in a large bowl and with a hand-held electric mixer, **whip** to **soft peaks**. Gently spoon the cream on top of the custard, top with the 50g raspberries and serve.

Coffee Panna Cotta
with Walnut Biscuits

Smooth and creamy coffee panna cotta is the ideal dessert for preparing ahead, served with the soft walnut biscuits and topped with chocolate-coated coffee beans.

For the panna cotta
6 sheets of leaf gelatine (see page 14)
200ml cold espresso coffee
100g caster sugar
600ml double cream

For the walnut biscuits
120g unsalted butter, softened
120g caster sugar
1 medium egg, lightly beaten
250g self-raising flour
1 teaspoon baking powder
60g walnuts, finely chopped

For the chocolate-coated coffee beans
25g dark chocolate
18 coffee beans

Needs a little skill

HANDS-ON TIME:
30 minutes

HANDS-OFF TIME:
4 hours or overnight chilling

BAKING TIME:
12–15 minutes

MAKES:
6

SPECIAL EQUIPMENT:
6 × 150ml capacity small pudding moulds or ramekins, 2 large baking sheets

1. For the panna cotta, soak the gelatine leaves in a bowl of cold water for 10 minutes to soften. Put the coffee and sugar in a small pan, and heat over a low heat until the sugar has dissolved. Stir the cream into the pan and heat again until the mixture is just beginning to simmer around the edges. Remove the pan from the heat.

2. Lift the softened gelatine leaves from the cold water and squeeze gently to remove the excess water, then add them to the pan and stir until completely melted. Put the pudding moulds or ramekins on a baking sheet and divide the coffee mixture between them – the level should come to just below the rim. Carefully put the baking sheet in the fridge to chill and set for at least 4 hours, but ideally overnight.

3. For the walnut biscuits, preheat the oven to 180°C (160°C fan), 350°F, Gas 4. **Line** two baking sheets with baking paper.
Continued

4. Put the 120g butter and 120g sugar in a mixing bowl, and cream together using a hand-held electric mixer until pale and fluffy. Add the egg and beat again.

5. Sift the 250g flour and 1 teaspoon baking powder into the bowl and **fold** in gently, add the 60g walnuts and fold again until the nuts are fully incorporated in the mix.

6. Take a teaspoonful of the mix, roll into a small ball and place on the baking sheet, pressing down the top lightly to flatten a little. Repeat with the rest of the mixture, leaving a 2cm gap between each biscuit as they will spread out as they cook.

7. Bake in the oven for 12–15 minutes until firm and golden. Leave to cool on the baking sheets for 5 minutes, then with a palette knife transfer the biscuits to a wire rack and leave to cool completely.

8. For the chocolate-coated coffee beans, place the 25g dark chocolate in a heatproof bowl to **melt** it, either in the microwave on a low heat, or set over a pan of gently simmering water, making sure that the bottom of the bowl doesn't touch the water (as it is such a small quantity of chocolate it is best melted in a microwave if you have one). Lay a piece of baking paper on your work surface or a flat board. Dip each of the 18 coffee beans into the chocolate and remove with a fork, letting any excess chocolate drip back into the bowl. Lay the beans on the paper and leave to set at room temperature (if you put them in the fridge to set the chocolate will develop a white bloom).

9. To serve, have a bowl of warm water to hand. Take the panna cottas out of the fridge and briefly dip each one in the bowl of water to help to release them from the moulds or ramekins. Dry the outside of the moulds and then turn out onto individual plates. Top each one with three of the chocolate coffee beans and serve with the walnut biscuits on the side. Store any leftover biscuits in an airtight container for up to 1 week.

Try Something Different

Make an orange panna cotta by replacing the coffee with 200ml freshly squeezed orange juice. Top with fresh orange segments instead of the coffee beans. You could also make the biscuits with the same amount of finely chopped hazelnuts in place of the walnuts.

Tiramisu
Gateau

Light sponge fingers, made by piping a **whisked sponge** mixture, are soaked in coffee and Marsala, then layered with a mascarpone mousse and topped with chocolate curls to create this impressive after-dinner dessert.

Needs a little skill

HANDS-ON TIME:
50–60 minutes

HANDS-OFF TIME:
12 hours chilling

BAKING TIME:
10–12 minutes

SERVES:
8

SPECIAL EQUIPMENT:
2 large baking sheets,
20cm springclip cake tin, piping bag fitted with a 1cm plain round piping nozzle

METHOD USED:
Whisked sponge,
pages 23–24

For the sponge fingers
4 medium eggs, at room temperature, separated
200g caster sugar
180g plain flour
2 tablespoons icing sugar

For the filling
3 medium eggs, separated
100g caster sugar
250g mascarpone cheese
150ml cold espresso coffee
75ml Marsala wine

For the topping
50g dark chocolate, ideally 60–70 per cent cocoa solids

1. Preheat the oven to 180°C (160°C fan), 350°F, Gas 4. **Line** two baking sheets with baking paper.

2. For the sponge fingers, put the egg whites in a mixing bowl or the bowl of a free-standing mixer and **whisk** until **stiff peaks** form. Add 130g of the caster sugar, a spoonful at a time, whisking well between each addition.

3. In a separate bowl, whisk the egg yolks with the remaining sugar until pale and doubled in size. Gently **fold** the yolks into the whisked egg whites, sift over the flour and fold again.
Continued

4. Use the mixture to **fill a large piping bag** fitted with a 1cm round piping nozzle and **pipe** fingers about 8cm long onto the lined baking sheets. You'll need about 40 in total. Space them well apart as they will spread as they bake. Dust the piped fingers with the icing sugar.

5. Bake for 10–12 minutes until golden. Leave to cool on the baking sheets for 10 minutes then use a palette knife to transfer to a rack to cool completely.

6. For the filling, put the 3 egg yolks and 100g caster sugar in a bowl and whisk until pale and creamy. Beat the 250g mascarpone cheese a little in the tub to soften it, then add to the egg yolks and mix together until blended and smooth. In a separate clean bowl whisk the 3 egg whites with a hand-held electric mixer

until stiff peaks form, then gently fold into the mascarpone mixture.

7. Remove the base from the tin (you won't be needing it) and butter and line the sides with baking paper. Set the ring on a serving plate. Mix together the 150ml coffee and 75ml Marsala wine in a shallow bowl.

8. Line the inside of the cake tin with a single layer of sponge fingers so that they stand upright around the edge. Trim the bottom of these fingers with a small, sharp knife so that the tops of the fingers just peep over the side of the tin. Place them back in the tin, right-side out and with the cut edge sitting on the plate. If you have trouble getting them to stay upright place a few pieces of scrunched up foil against them.

9. Dip the remaining sponge fingers one at a time in the coffee briefly on both sides, then cover the base of the serving plate inside the tin with a single layer of fingers, cutting some of them if needed to fill in any gaps. You want the whole of the plate inside the cake ring to be covered. Spoon one-third of the mascarpone mixture on top of the sponge fingers, then dip another batch of sponge fingers in the coffee mixture to create a layer on top of the mascarpone. Repeat with another layer of mascarpone and dipped sponge fingers and finish with the last of the mascarpone.

10. Cover the tin with clingfilm and put in the fridge to chill for 12 hours or overnight.

11. When you're ready to serve, carefully unclip the cake tin and lift off and peel away the baking paper. Use a potato peeler to shave the 50g dark chocolate into curls and sprinkle a thick layer on top of the gateau. Serve immediately.

Crème Caramel
and Orange
and Pistachio
Biscotti

Dark, rich caramel on top of creamy baked custard served alongside crisp, twice-baked orange and pistachio biscotti.

For the crème caramel
225g caster sugar
500ml full-fat milk
2 medium eggs, plus 4 medium egg yolks

For the orange and pistachio biscotti
200g plain flour
1 teaspoon baking powder
175g caster sugar
100g shelled and unsalted pistachios
2 medium eggs, lightly beaten
finely grated zest of 1 orange

HANDS-ON TIME:
40 minutes

HANDS-OFF TIME:
Overnight chilling

BAKING TIME:
25–30 minutes for the crème caramel, 45–50 minutes for the biscotti

MAKES:
6

SPECIAL EQUIPMENT:
6 × 150ml capacity ramekins, roasting tin, 2 large baking sheets

1. Make the crème caramel first to allow for overnight chilling. Preheat the oven to 150°C (130°C fan), 300°F, Gas 2.

2. Put 125g of the caster sugar in a pan and add 50ml water. Place over a low heat until the sugar has dissolved. Swirl the pan gently every now and then to help the sugar to dissolve evenly. Once you have a clear liquid in the pan increase the heat and boil until the sugar syrup turns to a deep caramel colour; again, swirl the pan once or twice once the caramel starts to form to stop it from burning round the edges (don't be tempted to stir the contents of the pan as you won't get a clear caramel). Pour the hot caramel into the ramekins and put to one side while you make the custard.
Continued

3. Heat the 500ml milk in a pan until it is just steaming, then take it off the heat. In a mixing bowl, **whisk** together the remaining 100g of sugar, the 2 eggs and the 4 egg yolks until combined. Gradually whisk in the hot milk, then pour the custard through a sieve into a jug.

4. Boil the kettle and put the ramekins into a roasting tin. Pour the custard over the caramel, dividing the mixture evenly between the ramekins. Pour water from the just-boiled kettle into the roasting tin so that it comes halfway up the sides of the ramekins.

5. Bake in the oven for 25–30 minutes until the custard is just set with a slight wobble in the centre. Remove the roasting tin from the oven and put the ramekins on a wire rack. Allow the crème caramels to cool completely before putting in the fridge and leaving overnight. This will allow the caramel to soak into the custard a little.

6. For the biscotti, preheat the oven to 180°C (160°C fan), 350°F, Gas 4. **Line** a large baking sheet with baking paper.

7. Sift the 200g flour and 1 teaspoon of baking powder into a bowl and stir in the 175g caster sugar and 100g pistachios. Make a well in the centre, then add the 2 eggs and finely grated zest of 1 orange. Use a wooden spoon to mix the eggs into the flour until it starts to come together to form a dough.

8. Turn the dough onto a lightly floured surface and knead gently just to bring together into a soft dough. Divide the dough into two equal pieces and roll each piece into a long sausage shape about 25cm long. Place both pieces on the baking sheet.

9. Bake for 25–30 minutes, or until golden and the base sounds hollow when tapped. Remove from the oven and put on a wire rack to cool for 15–20 minutes. Line another baking sheet with baking paper.

10. When the pieces are just warm, use a serrated knife to cut them into slices about 1.5cm thick. (If the biscuits are still too hot when you cut them they will crumble.) Lay the slices on the prepared baking sheet.

11. Bake for another 20 minutes, turning them over halfway through the baking time so that they turn golden brown on both sides. Remove from the oven and put on a wire rack to cool completely.

12. To serve the crème caramels, take them out of the fridge and run a small knife around the edge of each one to loosen the custard. Put a plate on top of the ramekin, then turn it upside down, give it a quick shake and lift off the ramekin, letting all the caramel drip onto the plate around the crème caramel. Serve with the biscotti. Store any leftover biscotti in an airtight container for up to 1 week.

Profiteroles with Salted Caramel and Chocolate Sauce

A chance to master choux pastry, these profiteroles are filled with a salted caramel crème pâtissière and topped with a rich, glossy chocolate sauce.

Needs a little skill

HANDS-ON TIME:
45 minutes

BAKING TIME:
20–25 minutes

MAKES:
18

SPECIAL
EQUIPMENT:
2 large baking
sheets,
2 piping bags,
plain round 1cm
piping nozzle

For the profiteroles
75g unsalted butter
1 teaspoon caster sugar
100g plain flour
3 medium eggs

For the salted caramel crème pâtissière
150g caster sugar
½ teaspoon sea salt flakes
2 medium egg yolks

3 tablespoons cornflour
300ml full-fat milk
200ml double cream, well chilled

For the chocolate sauce
150ml double cream
100g dark chocolate, preferably a minimum of 70 per cent cocoa solids, chopped
3 tablespoons golden syrup

1. Preheat the oven to 200°C (180°C fan), 400°F, Gas 6. **Line** two baking sheets with baking paper and prepare a piping bag with a 1cm plain round piping nozzle.

2. For the profiteroles, put the butter and sugar in a pan with 200ml water and heat gently over a low heat until the butter has melted. Bring the mixture to a vigorous boil, then remove from the heat and quickly tip in the flour and beat until smooth. Then put the pan back over a medium heat and cook for 1–2 minutes, stirring until the paste starts to come away from the sides of the pan. Spoon into a large mixing bowl and leave to cool slightly.

3. Lightly beat the eggs together in a jug and add to the dough a little at a time, beating well between each addition. The dough should be glossy and smooth with a soft dropping consistency. This means that if you hold a full spoon of batter above the bowl, the mixture will drop from the spoon. You might not need to add all of the egg, so check the consistency before adding the final bit. *Continued*

4. Sprinkle the baking sheets with a little water. This will create steam in the oven, which will help the choux buns to rise. Spoon the dough into the prepared piping bag to **fill** it and **pipe** into walnut-sized rounds, leaving a 2cm gap between them.

5. Bake in the oven for 20–25 minutes until golden brown and crisp. Remove from the oven and allow to cool slightly on the baking sheets. Then cut a small slit in the side of each one and put on a wire rack to cool completely. This allows the steam to escape as they cool and stops them from going soggy.

6. While the profiteroles are cooling make the crème pâtissière. Line a baking sheet with baking paper. Put 100g of the caster sugar in a pan with 2 tablespoons of water and heat over a low heat until the sugar has dissolved. Swirl the pan gently every now and then to help the sugar to dissolve evenly. Once you have a clear liquid in the pan increase the heat and boil until the sugar syrup turns to a deep caramel colour, again swirl the pan once or twice once the caramel starts to form to stop it from burning round the edges (don't be tempted to stir the contents of the pan as you won't get a clear caramel). Pour the caramel onto the baking paper, sprinkle over the ½ teaspoon of sea salt flakes and leave to harden and cool.

7. **Whisk** the 2 egg yolks and remaining 50g caster sugar together in a bowl until pale and thick, add the 3 tablespoons of cornflour and whisk again. Heat the 300ml milk over a low heat until just beginning to boil, then pour over the egg mixture, whisking all the time. Return the custard to the pan and slowly bring to the boil, stirring continuously. Simmer for a couple of minutes to cook the flour, then remove from the heat.

8. Blitz the hardened caramel in a food-processor to fine crumbs, then add it to the warm crème pâtissière and stir until all the caramel has melted. Spoon into a bowl, cover the surface with clingfilm to prevent a skin forming and leave to cool.

9. For the chocolate sauce, put the 150ml cream, 100g chocolate and 3 tablespoons of golden syrup into a small pan over a low heat. As the chocolate and syrup melt stir occasionally until you have a smooth thick sauce. Make sure that the sauce doesn't get too hot or the chocolate could become grainy. Pour into a jug.

10. Fit a clean piping bag with a 1cm plain round piping nozzle. In a large mixing bowl, **whip** the 200ml double cream for the crème pâtissière until it forms **soft peaks. Fold** the cooled crème pâtissière gently into the cream and spoon into the prepared piping bag.

11. To assemble the profiteroles, put the nozzle of the piping bag into the slit of the choux buns and fill each one with a generous portion of crème pâtissière. Pile them onto a serving plate, pour over the chocolate sauce and serve immediately.

Try Something Different

For a classic crème pâtissière simply leave out the blitzed caramel, or simply fill the profiteroles with 300ml double cream, whipped to soft peaks.

Hazelnut Meringue Gateau

Layers of crisp hazelnut **meringue** sandwiched together with fresh strawberries and softly whipped cream. A chance to try out your piping skills making the chocolate decorations.

Needs a little skill

HANDS-ON TIME:
45 minutes

BAKING TIME:
1 hour

SERVES:
8

SPECIAL EQUIPMENT:
2 baking sheets, small disposable piping bag, large piping bag, plain round 1cm piping nozzle, small palette knife

METHOD USED:
French meringue, page 28

For the meringue
4 medium egg whites, at room temperature
225g caster sugar
1 teaspoon white wine vinegar
1 teaspoon vanilla extract
1 teaspoon cornflour
75g toasted hazelnuts, ground

For the filling and decoration
50g dark chocolate
300ml double cream, well chilled
2 tablespoons icing sugar
300g strawberries

1. Preheat the oven to 120°C (100°C fan), 250°F, Gas ½. **Line** two baking sheets with baking paper.

2. Put the egg whites into a large mixing bowl or the bowl of a free-standing mixer and **whisk** until they form **stiff peaks**.

3. Add the caster sugar 1 tablespoon at a time, whisking well between each addition to make sure that each batch of sugar has dissolved before adding the next. Once you've added about half the sugar whisk in the vinegar, vanilla extract and cornflour, then whisk in the rest of the sugar as before. **Fold** in the hazelnuts.
Continued

4. Draw a 20cm circle on each piece of baking paper, turn them over and stick down to the baking sheets using a dab of meringue on each corner. Divide the meringue between the two baking sheets and spread each pile into a circle, keeping the tops as smooth as possible.

5. Bake in the oven or 1 hour until crisp and firm but not coloured. Turn off the oven, wedge open the door with a tea towel and leave the meringues to cool in the oven for another hour, this will stop them from cracking too much as they cool.

6. While the meringues are cooling make the chocolate decorations. Place the 50g dark chocolate in a heatproof bowl to **melt** it, either in the microwave on a low heat or set over a pan of

gently simmering water, making sure that the bottom of the bowl doesn't touch the water (as it is such a small quantity of chocolate it is best melted in a microwave if you have one). Pour the chocolate into a small disposable piping bag, snip off the very end to create a small hole and **pipe** shapes onto a piece of baking paper. You can either pipe the shapes freehand, or if you want something more even, draw your design onto the parchment first and follow the lines. Put to one side to set.

7. Prepare a large piping bag with a 1cm plain round piping nozzle. Put the 300ml cream and 2 tablespoons of icing sugar in a large bowl and **whip** the cream until **stiff peaks** form. Spoon about one-third of the cream into the prepared piping bag.

8. Slice 10 of the 300g strawberries in half, leaving the green tops on as they look more attractive that way. Leave three or four more strawberries whole, hull the rest and cut into thick slices.

9. Put one of the meringue discs onto a serving plate, spread the cream left in the bowl over the disc and top with the slices of strawberry in an even layer. Put the other meringue disc on top, pipe blobs of cream around the edge and a few in the middle.

10. Carefully lift your chocolate shapes off the baking paper using a small palette knife and place gently on the cream around the edge. Arrange the strawberry halves on top of the ring of cream and pile the whole strawberries in the middle. Serve immediately.

Brandy Snaps with Oranges in Caramel

The key to perfectly crisp brandy snap biscuits is to work quickly once they are out of the oven. They go beautifully with chilled orange slices in caramel to make a refreshing dessert.

For the oranges
250g caster sugar
6 large oranges

For the brandy snaps
60g unsalted butter
60g caster sugar
4 tablespoons golden syrup
60g plain flour
vegetable oil, for greasing

Needs a little skill

HANDS-ON TIME:
50 minutes

HANDS-OFF TIME:
Overnight chilling

BAKING TIME:
7–8 minutes

SERVES:
6

SPECIAL EQUIPMENT:
3 large baking sheets,
4 wooden spoons,
palette knife

1. First make the caramel for the oranges. Put the caster sugar in a pan with 50ml water and place over a low heat until the sugar has dissolved. Swirl the pan gently every now and then to help the sugar to dissolve evenly, resisting the temptation to stir the contents of the pan. Once you have a clear liquid increase the heat and boil until the sugar syrup turns to a deep caramel colour, again swirl the pan once or twice once the caramel starts to form to stop it from burning round the edges.

2. Remove the caramel from the heat and very carefully add 250ml water from a just-boiled kettle; the caramel may spit, so add the water slowly. Return the pan to the hob and heat gently until the caramel dissolves in the water. Pour into a heatproof jug and leave to cool while you prepare the oranges.

3. Holding an orange over a bowl to catch the juices, remove the peel with a small sharp knife (a serrated fruit knife works best here). Make sure you take off all the white pith with the peel. Cut the orange into thick slices and add to the juices in the bowl. Repeat with the other five oranges.

4. Pour the cooled caramel over the oranges, cover the bowl and chill for 12 hours or overnight for the oranges to absorb the flavour of the caramel.

5. For the brandy snaps preheat the oven to 190°C (170°C fan), 375°F, Gas 5. **Line** three baking sheets with baking paper.
Continued

6. Put the 60g butter, 60g caster sugar and 4 tablespoons of golden syrup into a small pan (warm a metal spoon in a mug of hot water first so that the syrup slides from the spoon). Heat gently over a low heat until the butter and sugar have melted and you have a smooth sauce. Remove from the heat, sift in the 60g flour and beat with a wooden spoon until smooth.

7. Put 4 teaspoonfuls of the mixture onto one baking sheet, spacing them well apart as they will spread as they cook (you'll need to cook these in batches as it will be hard to shape more than four brandy snaps at a time). Bake for 7–8 minutes until they are golden brown and have a lacy appearance. While they bake lightly oil the handles of four wooden spoons.

8. Remove the baking sheet from the oven and leave to cool for 2 minutes, then lift off the baking sheet using a palette knife and drape over an oiled spoon handle, with the top of the biscuit uppermost. Wrap the brandy snap around the wooden spoon, neatly but not too tightly or you might not be able to get it off when it has set. Repeat with the other three biscuits and leave to cool on a wire rack for about 5 minutes, then gently pull off the spoon and leave to cool completely.

9. Repeat with the remaining mixture, using a cold and clean baking sheet for each batch, to make 12 biscuits in total.

10. Serve the oranges chilled with the brandy snaps alongside.

Hot White Chocolate Souffles with Cardamom Shortcake

Test your whisking and folding skills with these light and fluffy hot soufflés served alongside crisp, delicately flavoured piped shortcake biscuits. If you'd prefer perfectly flat tops to your souffles, use straight-edged ramekins.

For the cardamom shortcake
12 green cardamom pods
200g unsalted butter, softened
100g caster sugar
200g plain flour
100g white chocolate

For the white chocolate soufflés
100g white chocolate
25g unsalted butter, plus extra for greasing
1 tablespoon plain flour
150ml full-fat milk
50g caster sugar, plus extra for coating
3 medium eggs, separated, plus
1 medium egg white, at room temperature

1. First make the cardamom shortcake. Preheat the oven to 180°C (160°C fan), 350°F, Gas 4. Fit a piping bag with a 1cm star piping nozzle.

2. Lightly bash the cardamom pods with a rolling pin to remove the seeds (discard the husks). Put the cardamom seeds in a pestle and mortar and grind to a fine powder. Put the butter and sugar in a mixing bowl and cream until light and fluffy. Sift in half the flour and the ground cardamom, and beat again. Sift the remaining flour into the bowl and gently **fold** in until you have a fairly stiff dough. Use the dough to **fill the piping bag**.

3. Pipe fingers about 6cm long onto the baking sheets, leaving a small gap between each finger. You don't need to line the baking sheets as the biscuits have such a high butter content they won't stick. Bake in the oven for 10–12 minutes, or until golden. Remove from the oven and leave to cool on the baking sheets for 5 minutes before using a palette knife to lift them onto wire racks to cool completely.
Continued

HANDS-ON TIME:
50 minutes

BAKING TIME:
10–12 minutes for the shortcake,
10–12 minutes for the soufflés

MAKES:
6

SPECIAL EQUIPMENT:
2 baking sheets,
piping bag,
1cm star piping nozzle,
6 × 150ml capacity ramekins

METHOD USED:
Creamed sponge,
pages 22–23

4. Melt the 100g white chocolate in a small heatproof bowl set over a pan of gently simmering water, making sure that the bottom of the bowl doesn't touch the water. Be careful not to overheat the chocolate as it will turn lumpy or grainy if it gets too hot. Put a sheet of baking paper on a wire rack. Dip one end of each biscuit in the chocolate, then put on the baking paper and leave to set.

5. To make the soufflés, preheat the oven to 200°C (180°C fan), 400°F, Gas 6. Put a baking sheet in the oven to heat up.

6. Melt the 100g white chocolate in a small heatproof bowl set over a pan of gently simmering water, then put to one side to cool.

7. Butter the ramekins well, then put a spoonful of sugar into each one and roll the ramekin around in your hand to make sure the whole of the inside is coated with sugar. Tip out any excess sugar.

8. In a small pan, melt the 25g butter and add the 1 tablespoon of flour. Cook over a gentle heat for 2 minutes, gradually **whisk** in the 150ml milk. Bring to the boil, still whisking, and cook for 2 minutes until the sauce is thick and smooth. Remove from the heat and whisk in the 50g sugar and then the 3 egg yolks, one at a time. Fold in the cooled melted chocolate.

9. In a separate bowl **whisk** the 4 egg whites until **stiff peaks** form. Add a spoonful of the whisked egg white to the chocolate mixture in the pan and mix in to loosen the mixture, then gently **fold** in the rest, just until no visible patches of egg white remain.

10. Fill a ramekin so that the level of soufflé mixture comes above the top of the dish, then take a palette knife and run an edge over the ramekin to scrape off any excess and leave a smooth, flat top. Run the tip of your thumb around the inside of the ramekin to create a small gap between the mix and the very top of the dish – this will stop the soufflé sticking to the ramekin and so help it to rise evenly. Repeat with the other five ramekins.

11. Place the ramekins on the preheated baking sheet and bake in the oven for 10–12 minutes until well risen and just golden on top; do not be tempted to open the oven door to check on them as they cook or the soufflés will collapse. Serve immediately with the shortcake biscuits on the side. Any remaining biscuits can be stored in an airtight container for up to 1 week.

Triple Chocolate
Gateau

A chance to master several skills, this impressive dessert layers chocolate genoise sponge with white chocolate and milk chocolate ganache, topped with a glossy layer of chocolate mirror glaze and caramelised hazelnuts.

For the chocolate genoise
75g unsalted butter, plus extra for greasing
6 medium eggs, at room temperature
160g caster sugar
120g plain flour
45g cocoa powder

For the milk chocolate ganache
250g milk chocolate, chopped
200ml double cream
25g liquid glucose

For the white chocolate ganache
250g white chocolate, chopped
200ml double cream
25g liquid glucose

For the mirror glaze
80ml double cream
100g caster sugar
40g cocoa powder
3 sheets of leaf gelatine (see page 14)

For the caramelised hazelnuts
100g caster sugar
40g blanched hazelnuts

HANDS-ON TIME:
45 minutes, plus chilling

HANDS-OFF TIME:
2 hours setting

BAKING TIME:
10 minutes

SERVES:
8–10

SPECIAL EQUIPMENT:
3 × 20cm sandwich cake tins,
2 large piping bags,
2 plain round 1cm piping nozzles,
baking sheet

METHOD USED:
Whisked sponge, pages 23–24

To make the chocolate genoise
1. Preheat the oven to 200°C (180°C fan), 400°F, Gas 6. Butter and **line** the bases of three sandwich cake tins with baking paper.

2. Melt the butter and put to one side to cool. Put the eggs and sugar in a large mixing bowl or the bowl of a free-standing mixer and whisk for at least 5 minutes until the mixture becomes very pale and thick and leaves a ribbon-like trail when the whisk is lifted.
Continued

3. Sift 60g of the flour and 20g of the cocoa powder onto the mix and gently **fold** in, taking great care not to knock too much air out. Sift over the remaining 60g of the flour and 25g of the cocoa and gently fold again, making sure you scrape right to the bottom of the bowl as the flour has a tendency to sink to the bottom when it's added. Pour the melted butter in around the edge of the bowl and fold in, again scraping to the bottom of the bowl.

4. Divide the mixture between the three tins – you want even layers, so weigh the filled tins to make sure you have put equal amounts in each one. Bake in the oven for about 10 minutes until firm to the touch and the cakes are starting to shrink away from the edges of the tin. Leave to cool for 5 minutes in the tins, then remove from the tins, peel off the baking paper and leave to cool completely on wire racks.

To make the milk chocolate and white chocolate ganache
5. Put the 250g milk chocolate in a large heatproof bowl. Heat the 200ml cream and 25g liquid glucose in a pan until just starting to simmer, remove from the heat and pour over the chocolate. Leave to melt for a couple of minutes, then stir until smooth. Using a **hand-held electric mixer**, whisk for about 5 minutes until the ganache is pale, smooth and glossy, and thick enough to pipe.

6. Repeat step 5 to make the white chocolate ganache. Prepare two piping bags with plain round 1cm piping nozzles and fill one with milk chocolate ganache and one with white chocolate ganache. Put both piping bags in the fridge for 30 minutes to firm up slightly while you make the mirror glaze.

To make the mirror glaze
7. Put the 80ml cream, 100g sugar and 40g cocoa powder in a pan and heat over a low heat until you have a smooth sauce and the sugar has dissolved. Increase the heat and simmer for 5 minutes, stirring occasionally, until the glaze thickens. Remove from the heat and leave to cool slightly.

8. Put the 3 sheets of gelatine in a bowl of cold water and leave to soak for 10 minutes. Lift the softened gelatine leaves from the cold water and squeeze gently to remove the excess water, then add to the chocolate and cream mixture in the pan and stir until the gelatine melts. Pour into a jug and leave to cool and set slightly for 30 minutes, stirring occasionally.

9. Line one of the cake tins with clingfilm and put one of the genoise sponges (the one with the smoothest top) into the tin. Spread the mirror glaze on top and put in the fridge and leave to set for a couple of hours.
Continued

To pipe the ganache

10. Take another of the genoise sponges (this will be the bottom layer), hold the piping bag of white chocolate ganache vertically upright and start piping neat round circles of ganache over the surface of the cake. Repeat with the third genoise sponge and the milk chocolate ganache and then return both piped sponges to the fridge to set a little (the ganache will have softened a little and it needs to be firm enough to support the weight of the cake layers).

To make the caramelised hazelnuts

11. Line a baking sheet with baking paper. Put the 100g caster sugar in a pan with 2 tablespoons of water and heat over a low heat until the sugar has dissolved. Swirl the pan gently every now and then to help the sugar to dissolve evenly (don't be tempted to stir the contents of the pan or you won't get a clear caramel). Once you have a clear liquid in the pan increase the heat and boil until the sugar syrup turns to a golden caramel colour, again swirl the

pan once or twice once the caramel starts to form so stop it from burning round the edges.

12. Remove from the heat and, working one at a time, put the hazelnuts into the caramel, remove with a fork and put onto the baking paper. If the caramel hardens as you work with the rest of the hazelnuts, put it back over a gentle heat to melt it again. Leave to set completely.

To assemble the gateau

13. Once all the layers are set put the white chocolate mousse-topped layer of sponge on a serving plate, carefully top with the milk chocolate layer and finally remove the mirror glazed layer from the tin and place on top. Decorate with the caramelised hazelnuts.

Baked Alaska

A strawberry ripple ice cream bombe creates the centre of this impressive classic dinner-party dessert, sitting on top of a light **whisked sponge** encased in **meringue**. The key to a successful baked Alaska is timing – it needs to be served straightaway.

Up for a challenge

For the strawberry ripple ice cream
600ml full-fat milk
1 vanilla pod, slit lengthways
6 medium egg yolks
225g caster sugar
600ml double cream, well chilled
300g strawberries

For the whisked sponge
2 medium eggs, at room temperature
60g caster sugar
60g plain flour

For the meringue
240g caster sugar
4 medium egg whites, at room temperature

HANDS-ON TIME:
45 minutes

HANDS-OFF TIME:
4 hours, plus overnight freezing

BAKING TIME:
17–20 minutes

SERVES:
8–10

SPECIAL EQUIPMENT:
Kitchen thermometer, 1 litre capacity pudding basin, 20cm sandwich tin

METHODS USED:
Whisked sponge, pages 23–24; Italian meringue, pages 28–29

To make the ice cream

1. Heat the milk and vanilla pod in a pan over a low heat until it starts to simmer. In a large mixing bowl whisk the egg yolks and 175g of the sugar together until you have a smooth paste. Slowly add the warmed milk to the bowl, whisking all the time.

2. Pour the egg mixture back into the pan and heat gently until the custard thickens enough to coat the back of a spoon. Remove from the heat and leave to cool. Once completely cold remove the vanilla pod.

3. Freeze the ice cream. To freeze ice cream without a machine, transfer the mixture to a wide plastic container with an airtight lid. You need the mixture to be no deeper than about 5cm, so you can beat it easily. Place in the freezer for 2 hours. Take the ice cream out of the freezer and scrape it into a bowl. Beat for a few minutes with a hand-held blender to break up the ice crystals. **Whip** the cream until **soft peaks** form

and **fold** this into the frozen custard, then return the mixture to the freezer container. Freeze for another hour, then mix well with a fork. If you have an ice-cream machine, it will churn the mixture as it freezes. Whip the cream to soft peaks and fold this into the chilled custard before transferring to the ice-cream machine – follow the manufacturer's instructions – then transfer to a plastic container with an airtight lid and store in the freezer for 1 hour.

4. Meanwhile, make the strawberry ripple. Put the strawberries and remaining 50g caster sugar in a pan and cook over a low heat until the sugar dissolves. Increase the heat and simmer for 5 minutes until the mixture thickens slightly. Push through a sieve to remove the seeds, put to one side to cool and then chill in the fridge until needed. Lightly butter the pudding basin and line it with clingfilm.
Continued

5. Remove the ice cream from the freezer, add the strawberry sauce and gently swirl it into the ice cream using a spoon to create a ripple. Spoon into the pudding basin and return to the freezer to freeze completely; this will take at least 4 hours but ideally leave it overnight.

To make the whisked sponge
6. Preheat the oven to 200°C (180°C fan), 400°F, Gas 6. Butter and **line** the sandwich tin with baking paper.

7. Put the 2 eggs and 60g sugar in a large mixing bowl or the bowl of a free-standing mixer and whisk for at least 5 minutes until the mixture becomes very pale and thick and leaves a ribbon-like trail when the whisk is lifted from the bowl.

8. Sift the 60g flour into the bowl and gently fold in, taking great care not to knock too much air out. Make sure you scrape right to the bottom of the bowl as the flour has a tendency to sink to the bottom when it's added.

9. Spoon the mixture into the tin, smoothing the surface as you go. Bake for 9–10 minutes until golden and starting to shrink away from the edges of the tin. Remove from the oven, leave to cool for 5 minutes in the tin, then put on a rack to cool completely.

To make the meringue
10. Put the 240g sugar in a pan with 60ml water. Heat over a low heat until the sugar has dissolved, swirling the pan gently to help the sugar dissolve. Once you have a clear liquid, increase

the heat and bring to the boil until the syrup reaches 120°C (250°F) on a kitchen thermometer. While the syrup cooks, **whisk** the 4 egg whites in a large, heatproof bowl with an electric mixer, or use a free-standing mixer with the whisk attachment, until **stiff peaks** form.

11. Preheat the oven to 200°C (180°C fan), 400°F, Gas 6. Put the ice cream bombe in the fridge for 15 minutes to soften slightly while you make the meringue.

12. Pour the hot sugar syrup in a thin steady stream onto the whisked egg whites, whisking all the time. Take care not to hit the beaters or whisk with the syrup as it will be hot and could burn if it splashes you. Once all the syrup has been added, carry on whisking the

meringue until it is smooth and glossy and cold. Scrape the sides of the bowl once or twice with a spatula to make sure you incorporate all the egg white.

To assemble the dessert

13. Put the sponge onto an ovenproof, flat serving plate, and turn the ice cream out of the bowl onto the sponge.

14. Spoon the meringue over the ice cream, making sure to completely cover both the ice cream and the sponge.

15. Once you have a thick, even layer, swirl the meringue lightly into a decorative pattern using a spoon or the tip of a skewer.

16. Bake for 8–10 minutes until golden all over. Serve immediately.

Millefeuilles

These delicate pastries require a little precision and care, and allow you to showcase several skills: layers of crisp **puff pastry**, smooth crème pâtissière and raspberry jam are all topped with feathered icing.

Up for a challenge

HANDS-ON TIME:
1½ hours

HANDS-OFF TIME:
2 hours 25 minutes
chilling

BAKING TIME:
30 minutes

MAKES:
4

SPECIAL
EQUIPMENT:
large piping bag,
plain round 1cm
piping nozzle,
2 large baking sheets,
small disposable
piping bag

METHOD USED:
Puff pastry,
pages 26–27

For the puff pastry
250g strong white flour, plus extra
for dusting
½ teaspoon salt
225g chilled unsalted butter
I teaspoon lemon juice

For the raspberry jam
100g fresh raspberries
100g granulated sugar
juice of ½ lemon
I tablespoon pectin

For the crème pâtissière
2 medium egg yolks
50g caster sugar
3 tablespoons cornflour
300ml full-fat milk
150ml double cream

For the icing
150g icing sugar
pink food colouring

To make the pastry

1. Put the flour and salt into a mixing bowl. Dice 25g of the butter and **rub** into the flour using your fingertips. Add the lemon juice and 150ml cold water and mix together with a round-bladed knife to form a soft dough. Tip onto a lightly floured surface and knead for 2–3 minutes until smooth. Put the dough in a clean bowl, cover with clingfilm and chill in the fridge for 30 minutes.

2. Place the remaining butter between two sheets of baking paper and use a rolling pin to press the butter into a square about 10cm across. Tip the dough onto a lightly floured surface and **roll** into a square about 20cm across. Place the square of butter onto the centre of the dough, positioned so that the corners of the butter are pointing at the middle of the sides of the dough. Take care not to handle the butter too much as this will soften it. Fold each of the corners of the dough over the butter so that they meet in the middle and encase the butter completely.

3. Give the dough a quarter turn so that a straight edge of the square is facing you. Make three indents in the dough with your rolling pin, across the top, middle and bottom of the square, and roll into a rectangle about 45 × 15cm. Then fold the bottom third up and the top third down, brushing off any excess flour from the pastry.

4. Give the dough another quarter turn and repeat the rolling and folding process. Wrap the pastry in clingfilm and chill in the fridge for 30 minutes.

5. Repeat the above rolling, folding and chilling process twice more, so that in all you have rolled and folded the dough six times. Chill for a final 30 minutes before using.
Continued

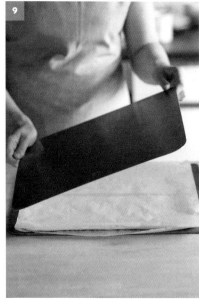

To make the jam

6. While the pastry is chilling make the jam and crème pâtissière. Put the 100g raspberries, 100g sugar, juice of ½ lemon and 1 tablespoon of pectin in a pan. Heat gently until the sugar has dissolved and then increase the heat, bring to the boil and boil for about 10 minutes until it reaches 105°C (220°F) on a kitchen thermometer. Put to one side to cool slightly, pass through a sieve to remove the pips and leave to cool completely.

To make the crème pâtissière

7. **Whisk** the 2 egg yolks and 50g caster sugar together in a bowl until pale and thick. Add the 3 tablespoons of cornflour and whisk again. Heat the 300ml milk over a low heat until just beginning to boil, then pour over the egg mixture, whisking all the time. Return the custard to the pan and slowly bring to the boil, stirring continuously. Simmer for a couple of minutes to cook the flour, then remove from the heat, spoon into a bowl and cover the surface with clingfilm to prevent a skin form forming. Leave to cool.

8. Prepare a piping bag with a plain round 1cm piping nozzle. In a mixing bowl **whip** the 150ml double cream with a balloon whisk or hand-held electric mixer until it forms **soft peaks**. **Fold** the cooled crème pâtissière gently into the cream and use it to **fill the piping bag**.

To bake the pastry

9. **Line** a large baking sheet with baking paper. Cut the block of puff pastry in half and on a lightly floured surface roll each half into a rectangle 36 × 15cm. Put both rectangles on the baking sheet and lay another piece of baking paper on top. Cover with the other large baking sheet on top of that, then chill for 20 minutes. Preheat the oven to 200°C (180°C fan), 400°F, Gas 6.

10. Bake the puff pastry rectangles for 25 minutes until golden brown, take off the top baking sheet and baking paper and bake for another 5 minutes until crisp. Cool for 5 minutes on the baking sheet, then carefully put on a wire rack to cool completely.

11. Using a serrated knife trim the edges of each piece of pastry so that they are nice and straight and then cut each piece into six even rectangles. Take the four best rectangles and set to one side to use for the tops.

To make the icing

12. For the icing, sift the icing sugar into a bowl and add enough cold water to make a stiff but spreadable icing. Take 1 tablespoon out and add a drop or two of pink food colouring, just enough to turn it pale pink. Spoon the pink icing into a small disposable piping bag and snip the end to create a small hole.

To ice the tops

13. Spread the white icing over the four top pieces of pastry, then **pipe** pink lines across the width of the pastry, about 1.5cm apart. Draw a cocktail stick lightly down the length of the pastry through the pink lines about 1cm in from an edge, draw another line going the other way down the middle, then a third line the same way as the first to create a feathered pattern. Repeat with the other three tops.

To assemble the millefeuilles

14. Spread a spoonful of jam onto each of the remaining pastry rectangles and then pipe lines of crème pâtissière onto each one, covering the jam. Layer up two jam and cream slices and top with an iced slice so that you have three layers in total. Serve immediately.

Trio of Tropical Desserts

Chocolate and passion fruit tart, lemon sorbet and a macarons filled with passion fruit cream make up this impressive trio, allowing you to master a number of different skills.

Up for a challenge

HANDS-ON TIME:
1½ hours

HANDS-OFF TIME:
2 hours, plus overnight freezing

BAKING TIME:
55 minutes

SERVES:
12

SPECIAL EQUIPMENT:
22cm round loose-bottomed fluted flan tin, 3 large baking sheets, piping bag, plain round 1cm piping nozzle

METHOD USED:
Rich shortcrust pastry, page 25

STORAGE:
Any extra tuiles and macarons can be stored in an airtight container for up to 3 days

For the lemon sorbet
300g granulated sugar
finely grated zest and juice
of 4 unwaxed lemons
1 medium egg white

For the chocolate and passion fruit tart
For the pastry
220g plain flour, plus extra for dusting
30g cocoa powder
50g caster sugar
125g chilled unsalted butter, diced
1 medium egg, lightly beaten

For the passion fruit custard
200ml double cream
75g caster sugar
60ml passion fruit juice
(from 6 passion fruit)
3 medium egg yolks

For the chocolate ganache
125g dark chocolate
225g milk chocolate
300ml double cream

For the tuile biscuits
2 medium egg whites
120g icing sugar
60g plain flour
60g unsalted butter, melted and cooled

For the macarons
80g icing sugar
80g ground almonds
2 egg whites, separated and ideally left in the fridge for at least 24 hours
80g caster sugar
orange food colouring

For the buttercream
50g unsalted butter, softened
100g icing sugar
1 tablespoon passion fruit juice

Note: This recipe uses uncooked eggs in the sorbet

To make the sorbet
1. Put the sugar in a pan with 600ml water. Place over a low heat until the sugar has dissolved. Increase the heat, bring to the boil and simmer for 2 minutes. Remove from the heat add the lemon zest to the pan and leave to infuse for 30 minutes. Pour the sugar syrup through a sieve into a shallow freezer container, add the juice, cover and freeze for 2 hours until it starts to go slushy.

2. Mix the sorbet with a fork to break up the ice crystals (this helps to ensure a smooth sorbet) and freeze again for another hour.

3. Whisk the egg white to soft peaks, mix the sorbet again to break up the ice and then **fold** in the egg white and freeze overnight.
Continued

To make the chocolate and passion fruit tart

4. First make the pastry. Sift the 220g flour and 30g cocoa powder into a bowl, stir in the 50g caster sugar, then rub in the 125g butter until the mixture resembles fine breadcrumbs. Add the egg and stir with a round-bladed knife until a dough starts to form. Bring the dough together with your hands, shape into a flat disc, wrap in clingfilm and chill in the fridge for 20 minutes. (Or make the pastry in a **food-processor**.)

5. **Roll out** the dough on a lightly floured surface into a circle large enough to line the flan tin and about the thickness of a £1 coin. Give the pastry a quarter turn every now and then to stop it sticking to the surface. **Line** the tin with the pastry, easing it into the corners, and run the rolling pin over the top of the flan tin to cut off the excess pastry. Press the pastry into the flutes of the tin with the side of your finger. Prick the base with a fork and chill again in the fridge for 20 minutes. This second chilling will stop the pastry from shrinking back as it bakes.

6. Preheat the oven to 200°C (180°C fan), 400°F, Gas 6. **Line** the pastry case with baking paper, then fill with baking beans or uncooked rice and **blind bake** for 15 minutes. Remove the beans and paper and bake again for another 5 minutes, or until the base feels dry and sandy to touch. Remove from the oven and lower the temperature to 180°C (160°C fan), 350°F, Gas 4.

7. While the pastry case cooks, make the passion fruit custard. Put the 200ml cream, 75g sugar, 60ml passion fruit juice and 3 egg yolks in a pan. **Whisk** together over a low heat until the custard thickens slightly. Pour into the cooked pastry case and bake for 10 minutes until just set with a slight wobble in the centre. Put on a wire rack to cool completely.

8. For the chocolate ganache, break the 125g dark chocolate and 225g milk chocolate into small pieces to allow it to **melt** evenly and place in a heatproof bowl. Heat the 300ml cream in a small pan until just starting to simmer, then pour over the chocolate. Leave for a couple of minutes, then stir gently until smooth. Leave to cool for 5 minutes, stir

again and then pour over the passion fruit filling. Put in the fridge for 2–3 hours until set.

To make the tuile biscuits
9. Put the 2 egg whites in a mixing bowl and lightly whisk until frothy. Sift in the 120g icing sugar and whisk again, then sift in the 60g flour, whisk, and finally the 60g cooled melted butter until you have a smooth mixture.

10. Put in the fridge to rest for 30 minutes. Preheat the oven to 170°C (150°C fan), 325°F, Gas 3. **Line** three baking sheets with baking paper.

11. Spoon a dessertspoon of the tuile mixture onto a baking sheet and spread into a thin disc. Repeat to make four discs on each sheet, leaving plenty of space between each one. Bake one tray at a time for about 10 minutes until they start to turn golden brown at the edges.

12. Have four small jars ready – spice jars are the ideal size – then slide a palette knife under each tuile and drape over the jars. Press the edges down to create a basket. You need to work quickly as the tuiles harden as they cool. Repeat with the rest of the mixture, using a cold baking sheet each time.
Continued

To make the macarons

13. Line two large baking sheets with baking paper. Put the 80g icing sugar and 80g ground almonds in a food-processor and pulse a few times to create a fine powder. Sift into a bowl to remove any large bits of almond, add one of the egg whites and mix to form a paste.

14. Put the 80g caster sugar and the remaining egg white in a heatproof bowl and set over a pan of gently simmering water, making sure the bottom of the bowl doesn't touch the water. Using a hand-held mixer, whisk for 3–4 minutes until you have soft, glossy peaks.

15. Take the bowl off the pan and whisk for 2–3 minutes until stiff glossy peaks are formed. Add the orange food colouring and whisk again until you have an even colour.

16. Fold the egg white into the almond paste – don't over fold, you want to just mix the two together until the mixture falls from the spatula in a thick ribbon. Fit the piping bag with a plain round 1cm piping nozzle and fill with the macaron mixture. Pipe onto the lined baking sheet into rounds about 2.5cm in diameter, leaving a 2cm gap between each one. Leave to rest for 30 minutes so that the macarons develop a skin – they should be dry to the touch before you put them in the oven. Preheat the oven to 170°C (150°C fan), 325°F, Gas 3.

17. Bake the macarons for 14 minutes until firm on the top and bottom, but still slightly gooey in the centre. Leave to cool for a couple of minutes on the baking sheet, then use a palette knife to transfer them to a wire rack to cool while you make the buttercream.

18. Put the 50g butter in a bowl and beat until soft and creamy. Add the 100g icing sugar a spoonful at a time, beating between each addition (small amounts will dissolve into the butter easily; if you add a lot of sugar at once the mixture can be dry and hard to work with). Add the tablespoon of passion fruit juice with the last spoonful of sugar and beat until smooth and creamy.

19. Spread a little of the buttercream onto the base of half the macaron shells and top each one with the other half; twist the two to spread the buttercream evenly and sandwich the shells together.

To serve
20. Take the sorbet out of the freezer about 10 minutes before you want to serve it. Cut the chocolate and passion fruit tart into slices and put on a plate with a macaron and a tuile basket. Just before serving, fill each tuile basket with a scoop of lemon sorbet.

Iles
Flottantes
Tart

A sweet **shortcrust pastry** case, filled with salted caramel and almonds, a creamy vanilla custard and clouds of marshmallow **meringue**, finished with a drizzle of caramel and flaked almonds.

For the pâte sucrée
125g unsalted butter, softened
90g caster sugar
1 medium egg
250g plain flour, plus extra for dusting

For the salted caramel
150g caster sugar
150ml double cream
15g unsalted butter
½ teaspoon sea salt flakes
100g toasted almonds, roughly chopped

For the vanilla custard
6 medium egg yolks
100g caster sugar
500ml double cream
1 vanilla pod, slit lengthways

For the marshmallow meringue
200g white marshmallows
4 medium egg whites, at room temperature

For the caramel and almond topping
50g caster sugar
15g toasted flaked almonds

HANDS-ON TIME:
1 hour

BAKING TIME:
45 minutes

SERVES:
10

SPECIAL EQUIPMENT:
23cm round loose-bottomed fluted flan tin, 3cm deep baking sheet

METHOD USED:
Pâte sucrée, page 26

To make the pâte sucrée
1. Put the butter and caster sugar into a mixing bowl and beat with a wooden spoon until soft and creamy. Beat in the egg and then sift in the flour and mix until you have a soft dough. Tip the dough onto a lightly floured surface and gently knead it a few times until smooth. Shape into a flat disc, then wrap in clingfilm and put in the fridge to chill for 30 minutes.

To make the salted caramel
2. While the pastry is chilling, make the salted caramel. Put the sugar in a pan with 2 tablespoons of water. Heat over a low heat until the sugar has dissolved. Swirl the pan gently every now and then to help the sugar to dissolve evenly, resisting the temptation to stir it. Once you have a clear liquid in the pan increase the heat and boil until the sugar syrup turns to a deep caramel colour, again swirl the pan once or twice once the caramel starts to form to stop it from burning round the edges.
Continued

3. In a separate pan heat the 150ml cream and 15g butter until it just starts to simmer. Once the caramel is golden brown turn the heat back to low and slowly add the hot cream. Pour it carefully as it will bubble and may spit. Once the sauce has stopped bubbling stir until smooth, then remove from the heat, add the ½ teaspoon salt, pour into a heatproof jug and leave to cool.

To prepare the pastry case
4. **Roll out** the dough on a lightly floured surface into a circle large enough to line the flan tin and about the thickness of a £1 coin. Give the pastry a quarter turn every now and then to stop it sticking to the surface. Use it to **line** the tin, easing the pastry into the corners. Run the rolling pin over the top of the flan tin to cut off the excess

pastry and press the pastry into the flutes of the tin with the side of your finger. Prick the base with a fork and chill again in the fridge for 20 minutes. This second chilling will stop the pastry from shrinking back as it bakes.

5. Preheat the oven to 200°C (180°C fan), 400°F, Gas 6. Put the flan tin on a baking sheet, then line the pastry case with baking paper, fill with baking beans or uncooked rice and **blind bake** for 10 minutes. Remove the beans and paper, and bake again for another 5 minutes to allow the base of the case to cook. Remove from the oven and put to one side to cool. Lower the oven temperature to 170°C (150°C fan), 325°F, Gas 3

6. Stir the 100g almonds into the salted caramel and pour onto the cooled pastry case. Leave to set while you make the custard.

To make the vanilla custard.

7. **Whisk** the 6 egg yolks and 100g caster sugar together in a mixing bowl until you have a smooth paste. Put the 500ml cream into a pan with the vanilla pod and heat gently until it just starts to steam. Remove from the heat put to one side for 15 minutes to allow the vanilla flavour to infuse the cream, then whisk into the egg yolks and sugar mixture until you have a smooth custard. Pour through a sieve into a jug.

Continued

8. Put the pastry case on its baking sheet on the middle shelf of the oven and carefully pour the custard over the base; pour it gently so as not to disturb the caramel layer. Bake in the oven for 25–30 minutes until the custard is just set with a slight wobble in the centre. Leave to cool on a wire rack completely.

To make the meringue

9. Put the 200g marshmallows in a heatproof bowl and melt on a low heat in the microwave. This should only take 30–40 seconds so watch them carefully as they hold their shape even when they have melted – check after 20 seconds and give them a stir. If you don't have a microwave you can set the bowl over a pan of very gently simmering water, making sure the bottom of the bowl doesn't touch the water.

10. Put the 4 egg whites into a large mixing bowl or the bowl of a free-standing mixer and add the melted marshmallows. Whisk on a high speed until thick and glossy and and have reached the **soft peak** stage.

11. Use a dessert spoon to scoop piles of meringue onto the cooled custard base, leaving a little gap between the piles.

To make the caramel topping

12. Put the 50g caster sugar in a pan with 1 tablespoon of water and place over a low heat until the sugar has dissolved. Swirl the pan gently every now and then to help the sugar to dissolve evenly (do not be tempted to stir the contents of the pan otherwise you won't get a clear caramel). Once you have a clear liquid in the pan increase the heat and boil until the sugar syrup turns to a golden caramel colour, again swirl the pan once or twice once the caramel starts to form to stop it from burning round the edges.

13. Remove the pan from the heat and use a teaspoon to drizzle lines of caramel over the meringue. Finish by sprinkling with the 15g flaked almonds and serve immediately.

What pudding or dessert shall I bake today?

Conversion table

WEIGHT		VOLUME		LINEAR	
Metric	**Imperial**	**Metric**	**Imperial**	**Metric**	**Imperial**
25g	1oz	30ml	1fl oz	2.5cm	1in
50g	2oz	50ml	2fl oz	3cm	1¼in
75g	2½oz	75ml	3fl oz	4cm	1½in
85g	3oz	125ml	4fl oz	5cm	2in
100g	4oz	150ml	¼ pint	5.5cm	2¼in
125g	4½oz	175ml	6fl oz	6cm	2½in
140g	5oz	200ml	7fl oz	7cm	2¾in
175g	6oz	225ml	8fl oz	7.5cm	3in
200g	7oz	300ml	½ pint	8cm	3¼in
225g	8oz	350ml	12fl oz	9cm	3½in
250g	9oz	400ml	14fl oz	9.5cm	3¾in
280g	10oz	450ml	¾ pint	10cm	4in
300g	11oz	500ml	18fl oz	11cm	4¼in
350g	12oz	600ml	1 pint	12cm	4½in
375g	13oz	725ml	1¼ pints	13cm	5in
400g	14oz	1 litre	1¾ pints	14cm	5½in
425g	15oz			15cm	6in
450g	1lb	**SPOON MEASURES**		16cm	6½in
500g	1lb 2oz	**Metric**	**Imperial**	17cm	6½in
550g	1lb 4oz	5ml	1 teaspoon	18cm	7in
600g	1lb 5oz	10ml	2 teaspoons	19cm	7½in
650g	1lb 7oz	15ml	1 tablespoon	20cm	8in
700g	1lb 9oz	30ml	2 tablespoons	22cm	8½in
750g	1lb 10oz	45ml	3 tablespoons	23cm	9in
800g	1lb 12oz	60ml	4 tablespoons	24cm	9½in
850g	1lb 14oz	75ml	5 tablespoons	25cm	10in
900g	2lb				
950g	2lb 2oz				
1kg	2lb 4oz				

Index

Acknowledgements

Hodder & Stoughton and Love Productions would like to thank the following people for their contribution to this book:

Jayne Cross, Linda Collister, Laura Herring, Alasdair Oliver, Kate Brunt, Laura Oliver, Joanna Seaton, Sarah Christie, Alice Moore, Nicky Barneby, Anna Heath, Damian Horner, Auriol Bishop, Anna Beattie, Rupert Frisby, Jane Treasure, Claire Emerson.

The author would also like to thank Laura Urschel and Katy Gilhooly for all of their help and support in the baking for the photographs, thank you. Huge thanks go to family, friends and neighbours and especially to Graham, Ben and Megan for eating all of my puddings and desserts.

First published in Great Britain in 2016
by Hodder & Stoughton
An Hachette UK company

1

Copyright © Love Productions Limited 2016
Photography & Design Copyright © Hodder & Stoughton
Ltd 2016

The right of Jayne Cross to be identified as the Author of the Work has been asserted by her in accordance with the Copyright, Designs and Patents Act 1988.

BBC and the BBC logo are trademarks of the British Broadcasting Corporation and are used under licence. BBC logo © BBC 1996.

A CIP catalogue record for this title is available from the British Library

Hardback ISBN 978 1 473 61550 2
Ebook ISBN 978 1 473 61551 9

Editorial Director: Nicky Ross
Editor: Sarah Hammond
Project Editor: Laura Herring
Series Editor: Linda Collister
Art Director: Alice Moore
Layouts: Nicky Barneby
Photographer: David Munns
Food Stylist: Jayne Cross
Props Stylist: Victoria Allen

Typeset in Dear Joe, Mostra, Kings Caslon and Gill Sans

Printed and bound in Italy by L.E.G.O. Spa

Hodder & Stoughton policy is to use papers that are natural, renewable and recyclable products and made from wood grown in sustainable forests. The logging and manufacturing processes are expected to conform to the environmental regulations of the country of origin.

Hodder & Stoughton Ltd
Carmelite House
50 Victoria Embankment
London EC4Y 0DZ

www.hodder.co.uk

Continue on your journey to star baker with tips and advice on how to *Bake It Better* from the **GREAT BRITISH BAKE OFF** team.

DON'T JUST BAKE. BAKE IT BETTER.